Walking
with
Grace

Walking with Grace

Embracing God's Goodness in Trauma

Grace Utomo
with Ivan Utomo

If you are looking for a prosperity gospel, happily-ever-after story, *Walking with Grace* is not for you. Though Grace and Ivan's story is punctuated with moments of light and hope, theirs is essentially a story of unimaginable suffering. And this is not a "rearview mirror" tragedy that is tied up with a pretty bow—they wrote this memoir while still sitting squarely in the middle of their pain, with no end in sight. Yet the breathtaking beauty of their steadfast trust in the sovereignty of God is what shines clearly through these pages. The resolute hope of these young people who have lost so much and yet still cling to their Savior is truly inspiring. Grace is a talented writer who tells a riveting story. Though their lives have certainly not gone according to anyone's plan, they bring much glory to God through their surrender to Him. This book is a gift to all of us.

AMY MEDINA: Former ReachGlobal missionary and current missions mobilizer; Writer at A Life Overseas and the EFCA blog

Walking with Grace is honest, riveting, heartbreaking, and encouraging, all at once. This is not a fairytale, but a picture of real Christian life. This book warns us that trusting our Sovereign God is no guarantee that tragedy will not find us, while reminding us that trusting in Him is the key to holding on to faith when tragedy does strike. The tapestry of God's providence that unfolds in these pages will be a healing balm to those who find themselves in the midst of a trial, and a guide to all who struggle to hold on to hope. In the end, *Walking with Grace* points to the hope we find in the One who endured suffering on our behalf, and how that truth triumphs over all.

DR. VODDIE T. BAUCHAM JR: Pastor and Conference Speaker

The most inspiring people I've ever met are those who trusted God to be faithful, even through the fire. Somehow they found a way to sing through the storm—believing that ultimately God hadn't left them to struggle alone. This is true of Grace and Ivan Utomo. *Walking with Grace* tells their intense story, and how they refused to give up on God, because deep down they knew He had not given up on them. They dared to believe that at some point there could even be beauty from the ashes. Shared so beautifully and honestly, this faith-filled book will bring fresh hope to many.

MATT REDMAN: Worship Leader and Songwriter

In a counter-narrative to the prosperity gospel, Grace and Ivan's journey from newlywed students and musicians through a life-altering trauma resulting in loss, mourning, and ongoing physical, mental, and psychological impairment, exposes the nature of faith's perseverance when God's answer to our persistent pleas for physical redemption is "My grace is sufficient for you." This narrative provides an inspiring example of faithfulness in an ongoing journey of hope in a merciful God who never promised a pain-free life in this world. It is evident that the Utomos' hope is in their confidence that they are not of this world.

WAYNE FLETCHER, EdD, MBA: Associate Provost, Academic Services; Associate Professor, California Baptist University, Riverside, CA

It's one thing to say we believe in the sovereignty of God, but another thing altogether to respond to horrific suffering with submissive faith in His never-ending goodness. *Walking with Grace* is an honest testimony of walking with God through indescribable pain and loss by clinging to His character and promises. It will encourage your heart, strengthen your faith in Christ, and grow your endurance no matter what kinds of suffering you may encounter.

PAUL TAUTGES: Pastor and Author

This book is a remarkable account of courage, love, and hope. Ivan and Grace's story is a dance with mystery and wonder. Like all music, the deepest meaning lies between the notes. The meaning lies in the silence between time and the search for truth. The wonder lies between the rigorous structure of imposed schedules and the surprise of unexpected grace. The mystery lies between numbing suffering and the resilient hope born of ever-deepening faith in a good and loving heavenly Father. Like a fugue, this story is woven together with rare honesty. Their story is not over, but this text gives the reader a glimpse into the mystery of providential grace and the wonder of eternal love. Read it and weep. Read it and be illumined by the light of joy.

Scott B. Key, PhD: Emeritus Professor of Philosophy, California Baptist University; Vice-President for Academic Initiatives, C. S. Lewis Study Center, Northfield, Massachusetts

Like so many young newlywed couples, Grace and Ivan set out full of excitement and anticipation of what their new life together would hold. Their lives were soon rocked by a catastrophic accident that left Grace in a coma with multiple bone fractures. God answered the prayers of family and friends that He would spare her life, but the road to recovery was fraught with many difficulties. In this work of self-revelation, Grace and Ivan share the spiritual lessons they learned in dealing with Grace's slow medical recovery, dealing with the medical profession, and also with other well-meaning people wanting to provide help. This recounting of their thoughts and feelings in navigating God's path for their lives is an extremely helpful, intimate look into what the hurting in the church experience. I would highly recommend this book to medical professionals, pastors, biblical counselors, and laypeople in the church to help equip them to care for people in a medical crisis.

Jonathan L. Scott, MD, PhD: General Internal Medicine Physician; Elder, Grace Community Church

As a hospital Chaplain for fifty-three years in three major hospitals in Los Angeles, CA, it has been my high and holy privilege to come alongside countless patients and their families in the direst of times. Rarely have I seen such a God-honoring pair as Grace and her husband. From the moment of the devastating, life-altering incident, their honesty, reactions, and biblical perspectives overrode even their own expectations of themselves. The team of experts coming and going surely had no idea of the underlying power and purpose this united pair seeking to love God and one another possesses. Their very personal journey shared helps any reader to recognize God's sovereignty and the fragility of life as they know it. It is obvious that Grace and her beloved husband have the desire to help others enhance their trust in God's goodness, no matter their circumstances of change and loss.

Rev. Phil Manly: Teaching Chaplain, Hospital Chaplains Ministry Association

This story of God's wonderful grace will allow you to walk alongside Grace and her family during this extremely difficult time in her, and her family's lives. It is a true story of my friend's daughter, a story of God's all-sufficient grace for Grace, a story of God's harmony within life's dissonance. Grace's words "God is able to heal me . . . but if He takes longer, or chooses not to heal me at all, God is still God, and absolutely, He's still good" are woven throughout the tapestry of her difficult days with a traumatic brain injury. This is a journey where God is helping Grace and her family focus on the upper side of God's tapestry in Grace's life. You will be blessed as you read about her journey, her growing faith, and her conformity to Christlikeness through her difficulty.

Stuart W. Scott, ThM, D.MIN: Director, The Center for Biblical Counseling; Professor of Biblical Counseling, BJU Seminary, Greenville, SC

Walking with Grace:
Embracing God's Goodness in Trauma
Grace Utomo with Ivan Utomo

Copyright © 2023 Grace Utomo with Ivan Utomo

ISBN 978-1-63342-311-4

Cover and book design and typeset by www.greatwriting.org | www.bestboutiquebooks.com

Shepherd Press
P.O. Box 24
Wapwallopen, PA 18660
www.shepherdpress.com

Find out more about Grace Utomo at www.walkingwithgraceweb.com
Printed in Colombia

Acknowledgments

"And though a man might prevail against one who is alone, two will withstand him—a threefold cord is not quickly broken."

Ecclesiastes 4:12

GRACE: Abundant thanks to my parents for their sacrifice in medical care, transportation, and temporary housing over the past seven years. Love to my sister, Anna, and her husband, Robert, for their willingness to swing by with a pot of soup or a box of "man tools" depending on what's broken. A special blessing on our brothers and sisters at Sunrise Church in Rialto, CA, who raced to the ER the night of December 3rd, 2016. Hallelujah for Hillside Church in San Jose, CA, who began supporting us even though they'd never met us, and continued blessing us with unconditional love and practical support for our first five years in Northern California. Much gratitude to my long-time mentor, Dr. Wayne Fletcher, for his intervention to secure me a place at Casa Colina Hospital. Warm thanks to the faculty at Savannah College of Art and Design, especially my thesis chair, Dr. James Lough. Praise God for my lifelong best friend, Grace Salyards, and for the brothers and sisters at City Light Bible Church, who prayed faithfully as I wrote. Love and gratitude to my brother, Tim Lee, for his constant encouragement and reminders to fix our eyes on Christ.

IVAN: Thanks to my parents, siblings, and extended family for their tireless love and support. I'm also incredibly grateful to the brothers and sisters at Christ Church of All Nations in Concord, CA, and at Calvary Chapel Old Towne in Orange, CA, for demonstrating God's care. Thanks to Robert Rubino and Iain Roush for their friendship and technical expertise in promoting this book. Thanks to Dr. Cliff Daugherty, Troy Gunter, Jeff Wilson, and the community at Valley Christian Schools for making our workplace an excellent place to experience and share the love of Christ.

❖

We both thank Jim and Sue Holmes and their colleagues at Shepherd Press for the faith, vision, and tenacity that brought this book to fruition. *Soli Deo Gloria!*

Foreword

Walking with Grace asks big questions like, is it really true that all things "work together for good to those who love God"? (Rom. 8:28, NKJV). What about when it seems God says no to prayers for healing and when pain speaks louder than words of comfort? Is it possible that a journey through the desert can ultimately give living water to millions dying of thirst?

When Grace Crosby's last name became Utomo, her marriage was seemingly "for better"—until a speeding white Mercedes crushed Grace's body onto the roadway in a crosswalk. "For better" suddenly became "for worse," and possibly "'til death do us part."

I've walked with Grace since her husband, Ivan, joined Valley Christian's Conservatory of the Arts as a beloved music instructor in August 2017. When tragedy strikes a family at our school, I often visit and pray with them. A few months after Ivan joined our staff, I also met with Grace's father, Pastor Keith Crosby, and learned that Grace's uncontrolled seizures might make an extended visit difficult.

Later, I began processing how similar Grace's story is to Job's. When God highlighted Job's faithfulness to Satan, Satan answered that Job was only faithful because God was protecting him. But God was so confident in Job's faith that He allowed Satan to attack Job in any way except for taking his life. During his suffering, Job declared, "Though He slay me, yet will I trust Him" (Job 13:15, NKJV). As I thought about Grace's inexplicable accident, I imagined God delighting in the faithfulness of Grace and Ivan while darkness covered their lives for so many years.

If you wonder how God loves in the face of tragedy and what faithfulness looks like when disaster strikes a godly couple, let's *Walk with Grace* together.

Dr. Clifford E. Daugherty: President of Valley Christian Schools and author of *Quest for Excellence, The Quest Continues,* and *Quest for Quality Education*

Introduction

Writing our story has taught me so much about my own failings, God's indescribable goodness, and the sacrificial love of my family and friends, that it's difficult to know where to begin. Thank you for taking this short walk with me!

During my acute recovery, shortly after I transferred from intensive care to a neurological rehab hospital, I remember telling a nurse I was going to turn our story into a book.

"Sure you are," she laughed. "That's what everyone says if they're lucky enough to survive and get accepted to our program. Then again, who knows? Maybe you will be the one who actually does it."

If I were simply writing a story about myself, there wouldn't be much to read. Being permanently disabled by a freak accident is sad—some might say tragic—but it is not unique. There are others who suffer equal, if not greater, losses every day. Rather than relating another Cinderella recovery story, my prayer is that somehow the following pages might approximate a fraction of the ways God intervened in my and my family's lives when trauma and disillusion should have wrecked our faith.

Much of this story is based on seven years of text messages, journal entries, and blog posts that I harvested back in 2021, hoping to shape them into a cohesive narrative. Other sections reflect the perspective God continues teaching me and my husband while we put the finishing touches on our book.

The writing process itself has been slow and roundabout: I've wanted to write many things that were not part of God's plan for this story, and God has guided me to share other things that I never intended to write. It's easy to churn out paragraphs of ol' faithfuls like "God works everything for good," or "Rejoice in trials," or "Forgive as you've been forgiven." But it's extremely hard to wake up every morning and follow Christ choice by choice when pain is real and nothing makes sense anymore. I have never and will never do it perfectly. I suspect I'm not the only one who feels ashamed to talk about these moment-by-moment battles in public. They sound weak and ungodly, like proliferating Doubting Thomas's.

But the truth is, God doesn't say yes to all our prayers. Sometimes we're left very, very confused, and our lives are still a mess, and we don't have the slightest clue what to do next. I began writing this story because I needed to figure out what to do after God said no to our desperate, years-long prayers for healing. And I wanted to encourage other people to start asking God their own questions with me.

God wants us to be honest with Him about our innermost struggles. The omniscient God already sees everything inside our hearts, but He still wants us to welcome Him as our Savior and Friend—not pretend we can leave Him outside banging at the door forever. He's more than capable of handling our hardest questions, confusion, and pain. God knows why He tells some of us no, and for what purpose. All we have to do is ask Him why with sincere hearts, and be willing to wait for His answer. The world wonders if we'll stumble beneath our trial. Sometimes, they may even assume our faith will collapse. But God, always there to help in times of trouble, promises to strengthen us so we keep walking with Him, whether or not our lives make sense in the moment.

That's why I wrote our story. To encourage you to ask God your own hard questions, to be honest with Him when trouble strikes, and trials hurt, and life no longer makes sense. Most importantly, I wrote our story to encourage you to keep writing yours. I encourage you also to fix your eyes on God's grace, both Jesus' sacrifice on the cross for our sins, and the Father's promise to provide your bread for today—spiritually and physically. May we all cling to the truth that God is working His perfect plan to glorify Himself in us, and that one day we'll see that plan fulfilled, whether here on earth or later in heaven, where we'll fall on our faces and cry together, "Hallelujah!"

Part One

December 3rd, 2016: Like Clockwork

I'm wrestling with my violin case on a chilly December afternoon. The strap refuses to cooperate, even when I switch shoulders. I refuse to give up. I need both hands for my satchel of Christmas music and I definitely need my wool coat for the fifty-degree weather. Ten unsuccessful minutes later I check my phone: *2:45 p.m.*

I can walk faster than Riverside traffic moves during rush hour, so I'm close to missing my call time if my new husband, Ivan, doesn't materialize soon. I need to be in Orange County by 5:00 p.m., and Orange County is ninety minutes away on a good day. What if I walk to the Subway where we'd agreed to meet and grab a pre-concert snack? Meeting him will only shave a few minutes off our drive, but anything is better than nothing.

At fourteen concerts in the next eighteen days, my Christmas schedule is the fullest it's been since I finished studying violin performance at the Eastman School of Music three years ago. It may even be overbooked since I'm also working a day job while Ivan finishes graduate degrees in piano performance and music composition.

I wrestle with my violin a few more minutes after checking my phone, then I grasp the case in my left hand and pray that I don't drop my overstuffed satchel with my right. Should I text Ivan to meet me at Subway? No. If he's running this late, I will text him once I get there.

I don't remember what happens next.

Footage from the security camera facing our apartment shows a car intercept me in the crosswalk after my pedestrian light flashes WALK. But the car isn't Ivan's blue Yaris. It's a white Mercedes. The Mercedes plunges through the red light and my skull shatters its windshield. Music flies everywhere. The driver throws the car in reverse, floors it, then slams on brakes a second time. My forehead and violin case smash the asphalt.

Doctors predict the severe traumatic brain injury, two strokes, and two brain bleeds will end my life that night. Ivan and I are twenty-three years old.

December 3rd, 2016: Missing

Neither of us remembers our goodbye that Saturday morning. My phone shows that I text Ivan a blurry selfie of myself with our kitten around 2:45 p.m. right before I leave the apartment. Am I apologizing for the breakfast tussle over our one working laptop? Why don't I mention Subway?

Ivan remembers calling me after his own concert ends at 3:15 p.m. I don't answer. He calls again. Still nothing. When he throws open our apartment door eight phone calls later, only our kitten bounds to meet him.

I rarely change plans without telling Ivan, and I'd never change plans before a paying gig. He hops back in our Yaris to check the Subway where we'd planned to stop on our way out. Maybe I headed there and forgot to text him.

An ambulance and fire truck block the intersection next to our complex, which does double duty as the entrance to California Baptist University and Ivan's U-turn into Subway. Sometimes he says a prayer for serious accidents, but this one doesn't look that bad—there aren't even damaged cars. He veers around the blockage, impatient to get to Subway.

My dad's name pops up on Ivan's caller ID just as he parks in front of the restaurant. Neither Ivan nor Dad makes social phone calls.

"Hello?"

"Ivan. What're you up to?"

"Um, nothing much."

"How's Grace?"

"She's fine. Why?"

"Well . . ." Dad clears his throat. "I'll get straight to the point. I've just heard from Doug Hall that he heard from a friend in CBU Public Safety that Grace has been in an accident. I think it's right at the entrance to CBU, you know, that crosswalk?"

"Oh, my goodness, I just drove by there and there was an ambulance and a fire . . ."

"As I understand it, they're already transporting her to the hospital. You find out what hospital and we'll get ready to fly down." My parents live seven hours north of Riverside in San Jose, California.

Ivan whips back onto Magnolia Avenue, but traffic is pulsing methodically where the ambulance was parked just minutes earlier. He opens the Life360 family locater app on his phone and sees my signal near Riverside Community Hospital. Why am I at the community hospital when we're insured through Kaiser Permanente? Did I forget to give them my insurance card? He doesn't know RCH has the only specialized trauma unit in Riverside County.

Not Part of the Plan

Ivan's Thoughts

When you are a young husband in your first year of marriage and your wife is missing when you are supposed to pick her up, and you call her phone many times but it always goes to voicemail, you start to worry.

When Grace's dad called me and said Grace had been in an accident, my heart skipped a beat. I'm usually pretty calm, but I could feel a panic starting to well up that I knew I had to control, if I was to keep functioning properly.

I had just driven past an accident, felt bad for whoever had been involved, and then driven on. In a split second, *it struck me that my wife was in that accident, that she was now in who knows what condition, and I had just driven by her mere yards away.* The panic sprang into full action.

I then realized I actually had no idea where my wife was. Well, she'd be heading to the hospital. But which one? There were two hospitals in Riverside: Kaiser, and Riverside

Community Hospital. They were in opposite directions. If I picked the wrong one, and if Grace was in critical condition, I would never forgive myself.

Somehow, I remembered to check the Life360 app, which showed that Grace was heading toward RCH. This was about ten minutes away.

I will never forget those ten minutes.

I prayed to God in a way I had never prayed before. *Oh God, PLEASE spare Grace! I know that if You allow her to die, she will be home with You in heaven forever, and she will be perfectly at peace and experiencing joy as never before. But I need her here with me, Lord! Please spare her life and let her stay on earth with me a little while longer! Let us experience life together as husband and wife. God, please spare her!*

My heart was pounding powerfully in my chest, and there was a buzzing pressure in my head. Sitting behind the wheel of my car, driving down Magnolia Avenue, I felt as though I was standing at the crossroads between heaven and earth. Some part of me knew that Grace could be all right, that perhaps she had only minor injuries.

But what really got me, what really made me feel as if the earth had given way beneath me, was the thought that by the time I made it to the hospital my wife could already be dead.

Suddenly death was not just a concept, not just something theological. It was not just something that happened to other people. It was a real presence, as real as if a person had been sitting in the back seat of my car.

I knew God was master over life and death. I knew Grace belonged to God. But I desperately, desperately wanted to see her alive, talk to her, be with her, if only for one last time.

April 17th, 2002:

A Dream and a Plan

Mom's threadbare Persian rug prickles my nine-year-old legs as I sit, mesmerized by the melodies pouring from our ancient TV. Two violinists face each other in front of the Israel Philharmonic, immersed in J.S. Bach's famous double concerto. One violinist doesn't look much older than me. The VHS jacket says his name is Itzhak Perlman.

My violin teacher lent me the tape as inspiration before my first violin competition since I'm also playing Bach's double concerto with another "promising" little girl. We win the competition, and I march into my lesson the following week announcing I'm going to be Itzhak Perlman when I grow up. Mrs. Elliott gently reminds me that only one person can *be* Itzhak Perlman, but I can be *like* him. I can even go to Juilliard like he did. She's never had a student who could go to Juilliard before, she whispers to Mom.

My parents' dial-up is as slow as its discount suggests, but that afternoon I navigate past Juilliard's graphics-laden home page to "Audition Repertoire" and write down every piece listed for prospective violin students. On top of my dream, I have a plan.

December 7th, 2011: Miracles Do Happen

It's the end of my first semester at the Eastman School of Music, the tiny school in Rochester, NY, that's outranked Juilliard three years running. I'm grinning like a toddler as my left hand ghost-fingers a concerto on my violin. My professor and I always face each other during my lessons: I'll be balancing asymmetrically in performance stance, most of my weight slung on my left foot, while Mr. Castleman fidgets merrily in his cherrywood rocker, curly grey head nodding with the music. Occasionally, he might snatch his violin from the dilapidated card table to his left and demonstrate a passage, but he dislikes this approach. Mr. Castleman prefers discussing ideas and letting me synthesize my own solutions.

Perhaps my ability to generate my own musical ideas has catalyzed what I consider to be an unlikely relationship. As one of the school's top violin professors, Mr. Castleman ignores the virtuosic pageantry most students exude. He selects a couple of freshmen annually, and his decisions are final. My old violin teachers might have insisted that innate musicality and work ethic will equalize the prohibitively expensive world of rising artists, but freshman orientation at Eastman convinced me otherwise.

It was barely seventy-two hours after our scuffed, red Camry vanished at the end of Gibbs Street before I was sick of my classmates' questions: "What does your father do?" (*Nothing. . . . I mean, not right now . . . he's looking for a job*). "Where are you from?" (*Georgia. I guess technically I live in Wisconsin. We move around a lot*). "Who was your high school violin teacher?" (*Do you know Samantha George? Oh well, she's really great.*) My make-it or break-it audition might have been inspiring on the Hallmark channel, but it was a social death sentence in real life. I quickly grew too self-conscious of my rural high school résumé to comprehend how I'd been accepted to the school, much less to Mr. Castleman's studio. I ignored the exhibition to avoid inserting myself where my classmates—the US kids who win national competitions, and the foreign ones who move to the States to attend school—insinuate that I will fail.

Yet, somehow, I've reached the final lesson of my first semester. Mr. Castleman is rocking in his chair, gnarled fingers drumming as usual, oblivious to my exuberance. After all, I was in his office only a couple of weeks ago sobbing over my scholarship. My dad had been looking for full-time work for eight months and I had just submitted my withdrawal paperwork, even though I had been working weekday nights—working instead of practicing.

"How are you today?" Mr. Castleman is not about to investigate my mood swing. He had already checked his "cordial" box so he could proceed to the "make student play repertoire" box.

"I'm GREAT!" I explode. "I don't know how it happened, but I'm not leaving. A lady from Financial Aid called me all mysteriously yesterday and made me come to the office and . . . I thought it was to sign more withdrawal forms, but it turns out they have found someone to sponsor me for the rest of my degree. Except I had to sign this nondisclosure thing since apparently it was top secret or something. She said no one gets more than a 60 percent scholarship here, ever." I pause. Mr. Castleman would know the answer since he's culled Eastman's top players for decades.

"Very true." He still seems nonplussed by my reversal. Considering he had selected my underwhelming self over countless other more dazzling candidates, I'd expect him to look at least a little relieved that he's not losing his investment. What if he'd been counting on my withdrawal to make room for one of those *real* prodigies? I scan the room for a distraction from this supposition, finally landing on his crimson red and black "WWND?" sign. "What Would a Ninja Do?" What *would* a ninja do right now? I draw a blank.

"Of course, you're staying." He jerks his shoulders and grins. "*What*?" My left hand stops ghosting the concerto on my violin.

"I went to the Dean and told him he couldn't let you go. Now about January. What do you think of Ysaÿe's *Ballade*?"

I nod cautiously. As much as I love the *Ballade,* I've only heard of graduate students attempting it. I'm eighteen. Is this a test? Or does he believe in me that much?

August 17th, 2012: Strings Attached

Mr. Castleman's office is stifling. The August humidity soaks his Hawaiian polo to his torso and plasters my left hand to my violin, prohibiting me from wiping it on my jeans before I play. My mind drifts to the donors' aerated marble lobby downstairs. Just how long can Eastman's administration ignore the faculty's un-airconditioned offices?

"So how did you like Catherine?" Mr. Castleman whizzes over to a sagging shelf by the window and pries open a damp étude book. He seems immune to the humidity.

I drag my thoughts back to my impending doom. "Well, if I'm being honest . . . we didn't exactly get along." I'd declined his recommendation to attend a summer music festival, even though most students visited at least one per vacation to keep themselves sharp. My parents and I were followers of Jesus Christ; as Christians, we believed God wanted me to prioritize worshiping Him and investing in my family over future career plans. And so I spent the break at home, attending and serving at church with my parents and younger sister.

In a sweeping gesture of forgiveness for wasting my summer in California, Mr. Castleman had convinced the concertmaster of the Recording Arts Orchestra in Los Angeles to meet me for coffee, maybe even mentor me. Catherine's position leading this ensemble would be a dream gig for many violinists: orchestra contracts are hard to come by, and the Recording Arts Orchestra lays down all the soundtracks for Sony Picture's films. Nevertheless, here I stand, the week before school, sweating profusely and reporting that my mentor wasn't a good fit. My worthlessness blankets me closer than the dripping Rochester heat.

"Catherine left her husband and kids because they kept interfering with her recording schedule," I falter. "I think she even went like two weeks without seeing her kids one time while she was married." Hopefully, these details help my case. We both know I skipped summer festivals specifically to see my family.

Mr. Castleman shrugs and plops back in his chair, still fidgeting with the étude book. I can't comprehend why he teaches from a rocker when he exudes triple my energy, in spite of our fifty-four-year age difference.

"I had a student once who got married. Big mistake. Ruined her career."

I cringe. Did he select this mentor to address what he considers a debilitating flaw? I'm painfully aware how much I owe him after my scholarship. The least I can do is make a decent name for myself. Does that require walking out on my family? There are some prices I won't pay—not even for him.

"Well, there is one other thing." No matter where we stand on my first objection, I'm positive we'll agree on this one.

"Which is?"

"I want to end up in California with my family. I mean . . ." I rush to cover my lapse. ". . . I'm fine with touring, but something like Catherine's recording job would be great when I'm ready to settle down . . . *after* I'm done touring, that is."

"And?"

"She basically said there was no way I could get a job, even coming from Eastman. She said the market's too competitive and I didn't look like I had what it takes." Now it's my turn to fidget, inducing a cough-worthy cloud of musk from the ancient shag carpet. "And you know, she's probably right. If you think about all the people coming out of here and Juilliard. That's a lot of people, not to mention the pros who've been around forever. And who am I kidding about touring with a chamber group?" I accelerate as I begin reciting the incompetence I've internalized from my mother. "I don't have perfect technique. And I can't afford a fancy violin like everyone else. Basically, there's a ton of people who sound better than me."

Mr. Castleman tosses the étude book on a nearby desk, still fiddling with his hands in his lap.

"Did she hear you play?"

"Well . . . no."

"First, good people always find jobs. And good people don't need fancy instruments to find them. So, forget about that. Second, when people get here, I already have a plan for them. I know how good they are, what I'll do with them, and how far they'll go after they graduate. But with you, I don't know. I had a plan when you showed up last year, but with how you've been improving over the past few months, I really have no idea."

Direct compliments from Mr. Castleman are rare. I've never received compliments skillfully from anyone. But praise from the man who's coached premier violinists makes me feel like an alien.

Fall 2012: A Change of Heart

Mr. Castleman's confidence transforms me from an anxious freshman hiding in the back of the second violins to one of four sophomores who rotate sitting concertmaster during orchestra concerts. My weekends fill with lucrative gigs serenading Rochester's elite upper class. I join a community orchestra eager for ringers who play like professionals and charge like students. Best of all, my school performances morph from embarrassing to exciting.

But the more I succeed, the less I celebrate. I'd spent most of that freshman summer locked in my bedroom practicing instead of going on family adventures as I'd promised. Now that I'm back in Rochester, I skip evening church services to practice for the week ahead. My conflicted interests climax when a young mom from church calls to ask if I'll babysit so she and her husband can celebrate their anniversary. "I'm so sorry, but I'm already booked," I lie. I'd rather not push my homework to tomorrow and lose an hour of precious practice time.

Jesus' words stab my heart the minute I hang up: "*You must love the Lord your God with all your heart, all your soul, and all your mind. This is the first and greatest commandment. A second is equally important: Love your neighbor as yourself*" (see Mark 12:29-31). Should I call her back? I'm here to get my education, not volunteer as a church babysitter. "*If any of you wants to be my follower, you must give up your own way, take up your cross daily, and follow me*" (see Mark 8:34). I don't call the lady back, but I say yes the next time I'm asked to babysit. *Would you have said yes on your own?* This family asked me and my best friend to babysit together. I have no idea what I'd have said by myself.

These incidents may seem relatively harmless but they're not isolated. And they feel enormous to a heart already guilty from sidelining my family all summer. Late one night in my overheated dorm room, just after Thanksgiving, I realize what I have to do. Maybe mature students can keep their priorities in order, but I'm acting like I worship the violin. If I really want to call myself a Christ follower, I need to go somewhere I'm not tempted to ignore Him at every turn. Even if that means leaving my dream school.

"Are you *sure* you're sure?" Mom remonstrates. "Even with the scholarship?"

"If you're leaving Eastman, you better major in something that actually makes money," Dad warns. "You know how hard elite musicians struggle to support themselves, much less the ones coming from no-name schools." I promise to pick something lucrative, and he agrees to write Mr. Castleman a formal letter explaining my withdrawal.

I'm too heartbroken to read it.

In truth, I'm too heartbroken to think about my withdrawal at all. Mr. Castleman and Eastman become a black hole in my life that no one dares mention. One look back and I know I'll go crazy for leaving the school and the dream that's absorbed thirteen years of my life. It won't matter that I felt God was calling me to leave.

I don't mention Eastman again for almost five years.

In January 2013, I begin classes at California Baptist University. The assistant to the registrar, who attends my dad's church, notified the School of Music that they might score an ex-Eastman student if they offered a generous scholarship. We negotiate a scholarship with two conditions: I'll work with the school's seminal strings program if they'll allow me to major in healthcare administration.

November 12th, 2013: To Date or Not to Date

Eleven months after I transfer from Eastman, I perform as a soloist with CBU's Symphony Orchestra. This is the first time the symphony is accompanying a soloist, and the conductor selects a simple piece sure to be an audience favorite. I've performed the theme from *Schindler's List* several times over the years so I don't pay much attention in rehearsals until I get a mysterious text two weeks before the concert.

> **925-822-4959:** Hey, Grace, you sounded great in Symphony today!
>
> *Me:* Thank you! ! I got a new phone . . . who is this? !
>
> **925-822-4959:** This is Ivan!
>
> *Me:* Haha, hi Ivan! !

Ivan plays the piano for the School of Music's two best choirs. He's also its most desirable bachelor, thanks to his meticulous recitals, entertaining musical improvisation, and unlimited empathy for girls' post-lesson meltdowns. But I've never heard of him singling someone out.

I decide the text is too random to be significant, even if Ivan went to a bit of trouble getting my number. But there's no way to explain him catching me fifteen minutes before my *Schindler's List* performance and asking me to dinner. Only me.

A couple of weeks before the concert, I'd hosted him and an international student for Thanksgiving. A few days before the concert, he'd invited me to see the school production of *Much Ado About Nothing* with him and some mutual friends. The show falls the day after I solo with the symphony, and I've almost forgotten about it in light of the concert or because I refuse to be desperate for Ivan's attention. Either way, I'm completely unprepared when he finds me backstage and invites me to dinner before the play.

I rattle off a list of reasons to justify my "no":

- I don't have a meal plan since I live off campus.
- The school dining center is too expensive.
- He's already paid for my ticket to the show.

Ivan blinks sheepishly and wanders away. My gut says I've done something wrong, but I'm not sure just what.

Preparing for a performance is like preparing for a sporting event. I need those final minutes to focus, sneak in some extra mental practice. But I've never been asked on a date before. Now is the absolute worst time to up our friendly hangout to a "dinner-and-a-show." But Ivan can't know that.

All this information cycles through my head as I stand before the orchestra in my black gown, filling the centuries-old church with heart-rending melodies from *Schindler's List*. My solo opens the concert. Afterward, I wade back to my normal seat in the first violins and spend a Beethoven symphony wallowing in consternation. *What should I do?* No guy wants to be rejected within earshot of an orchestra of fellow students. An apology is probably the correct response. If only God would grant me a less embarrassing way to patch things up! He doesn't.

"So, Ivan," the gold pattern on the church's crimson carpet is surprisingly intricate, "I just wanted to say it was really nice of you to invite me to dinner." The pattern is truly fascinating—perhaps as old as the nineteenth-century building itself. "I guess you've probably got other stuff to do before the show, but I could still meet you at the dining center if you're up for it." I brace for the inevitable as I force my eyes to meet his.

"Yes." He smiles and wanders away.

What in the world will I do on a real-life *date*?

December 30th, 2015: Till Death Do Us Part

"It's a shame you look this beautiful! It'll all be downhill from here." Mom is pinning my wedding veil in place. Its cathedral-length, ivory tulle is perfect for the wedding chapel at the Mission Inn, a luxurious, nineteenth-century hotel just a couple of miles from my parents' house.

"Mom! You're so depressing."

"You know I'm teasing!" Mom takes the last pin from her mouth and buries it in the elaborate braid woven beneath my tiara. "I'm sure you'll look gorgeous for years to come. Especially since you're just twenty-two." She fluffs my veil again, then steps aside for the photographer.

Our Wednesday-morning wedding does feel like a fairytale, complete with stained glass windows and a golden chandelier. Ivan and I are confident this union is God's will for our lives, even though we've been warned the marital odds aren't in our favor. Why not stay casual since we're so young, some friends and family suggest. Neither of us want to wait. Ivan and I have spent the past eighteen months praying for wisdom, and God affirmed our prayers by providing jobs so we could support ourselves, even though some musicians struggle into their thirties. If God has enabled us to get married, then He'll keep us together even when we want to quit. *"For better and for worse . . . in sickness and in health . . . till death do us part."*

December 3rd, 2016: Stage Fright

Savvy performers silence their cell phones. It's a reflex. My sister, Anna, is giving her phone its third and final check when she sees Ivan's voicemail. If there is one thing my sister hates, it's listening to the same message she could read in a text. Doesn't Ivan know today is the Chamber Singer's first Christmas concert? Then she pauses. If Ivan left a voicemail, he probably had a reason. She hits play but all she hears is a muffled intercom. Then:

"Hey Anna, I know you're at a concert right now, so . . . uh . . . sorry I'm interrupting, but . . . Grace was in an accident." Ivan's voice is wobbly and distant. "Can you come? I just got to RCH."

Anna closes her eyes, too confused to panic. "Accident" could mean anything. Something's wrong about "car accident," but she isn't sure what. Or maybe it's the fact I'm alone. Going anywhere by myself on the weekend is odd since Ivan and I are still inseparable newlyweds. She combs her memory for clues about why we would've been apart that afternoon.

The auditorium's flashing lights snap her back to reality: Five minutes until the concert's downbeat. Anna grabs her black leather jacket off the pile by the green room exit, then corners the conductor who's already hovering near the stage entrance.

"Excuse me." Anna cuts an imposing figure at 5'11" and concert black makes her especially formidable. "My sister has been in an accident."

"Can't you see? We're starting in three minutes!" her professor snaps. "Who else is supposed to play the piano? You need to think about more people than yourself, young lady. I'm sure your sister can survive another hour!"

"I said I'm going." The singers huddled near Stage Right stop whispering.

"Shh! Hold on a sec!" The conductor's husband sticks his head around the curtain.

Apparently, the audience can also hear the controversy. "I saw an ambulance and a fire truck at the main entrance an hour ago."

"Well, *was* there a car?" "I didn't see one, but . . ."

Anna tosses her music to the nearest singer before he finishes.

December 3rd, 2016: Rules Are Subjective

"Right this way." The ICU nurse beams as she guides Ivan and Anna into the Level IV trauma unit at Riverside Community Hospital. Ivan's shoulders sag beneath his overstuffed backpack. Anna wonders if all ICU nurses smile this hard.

I'm in a coma.

It's only been ninety minutes since Ivan and Anna saw me in the emergency room, but I've transformed from a slender twenty-three year-old into a balloon of blanched flesh. A respirator protrudes from my taut lips and IV ports appropriate most available veins, including a large one in my neck.

Ivan wills himself to look at Anna. "Umm . . . maybe go meet your parents when they get here. They're gonna need to be prepped before they see this." He gestures to an official looking placard near the clock on the wall. "It says only two at a time. I guess we'll take turns once they're here."

"No, not at all!" the nurse chirps as she continues hooking me up to various machines. "You got friends and family out there? You can have as many people as you want!" Anna and Ivan exchange confused glances. Rules blocked them at every turn when they tried visiting me in the ER; now they're in the hospital's most specialized unit and the nurse is ignoring an extremely obvious sign. But neither has the energy to ask questions. Ivan mumbles that they're waiting for my parents, then drops his backpack and slumps into a blue silicone chair. Anna begins pacing.

Mom bursts into tears when she and dad round the corner to my room. The nurse gives them a moment to steady themselves before piping up again:

"Please, go get the whole family! We can fit a lot of people in here." Unlike Ivan and Anna, my parents know exactly what she means. No rules mean no life expectancy. Mom shakes her head as reality slurs her thoughts. "All our family . . . lives in Georgia . . ."

The nurse blinks. "Hmm. Well, you got friends out there? Promise it's fine for them to come too!" Dad nods to Anna. She glides back to the waiting room and returns with her roommate.

"Let us pray," Dad pronounces, and they form a circle around my bed. Two nurses join them silently.

December 4th, 2016: Viral

Ivan announces my accident on Facebook a few hours later. No one imagines his post will blossom into a daily series followed by friends and family on both sides of the Pacific:

As many of you may have heard, yesterday, my wife, Grace, was hit by a car as she was walking across the crosswalk on Magnolia Ave heading towards CBU. She was taken to the ER. Initially, she was stable and responsive but her mental responsiveness took a downturn, and she needed to be put in a coma and on a breathing tube, and transferred to the ICU. She has a fracture in her skull, bleeding in her brain, a shattered left knee and fractured right knee, and fractured pelvis. They have done multiple CAT scans on her and we are waiting for the neuro doctor to confirm that her brain has stabilized enough for them to do surgeries on her knees. Please pray. I am so thankful for all who have let me know that they are praying, I can't express how much that means to me and to Grace's family! Our God is sovereign and gracious, and we want to entrust Grace completely to Him. May His will be done!

December 2016: Canceled Concert

What time is it?

I open my eyes, savor my woolen cocoon.

I should take more naps. Then I see the ceiling. We don't have a tile ceiling or fluorescent lights.

The concert!

I'm going to be late. I try jumping out of bed but nothing moves. Suddenly, Ivan's face appears. It's almost touching mine.

"Where am I?"

"You've had an accident. Everything's going to be okay." He tells me that I repeat this cycle for days.

I have no idea.

December 2016: Floating

Light gradually unsettles the narcotic fog, but Ivan's Facebook updates are the only real key to deciphering my brain-injured reality as I wake up:

12/11/16: Today the doctors, nurses and staff at Kaiser Fontana spent the day getting to know Grace. They ran tests on her, did scans, asked her questions, gave her pain medication . . .

She had a tiny bit more success with words, although we still have a hard time understanding the sounds she makes when she's trying to talk. It is such a burden for us to watch Grace be trapped in her own body and mind. But here we turn to God's sovereignty and unchanging grace.

Ivan claims that he sleeps next to my bed, but he's only faking so he can sneak out and get high on street drugs at that Japanese tea house across the street. Two nights ago, he dragged me with him so some waiter could force me to inhale smelly fumes while Ivan passed out on a couch. Doesn't he know I'm supposed to stay in the hospital? Last night, the nurse caught me throwing pillows at Ivan so he wouldn't do it again. Someone tied my hands to the bed.

12/12/16: The speech therapist came by to do the swallow evaluation on Grace again (to see if she can swallow safely on her own and be able to eat and drink), but Grace had just been given pain medication and was asleep.

Urgent prayer request: Grace only has one more chance to pass the swallow evaluation . . . if she doesn't, they're going to need to put a feeding tube (NG tube) down her throat, and I know she would not want that at all.

Owls were my favorite part of the Hogwarts Hotel. But I wish someone would get rid of the one hanging in the cage behind my head now that I'm home. Its whirring keeps me up at night. Or maybe I'm allergic. Why else are knives slicing my throat?

"There's no owl, sweetie," the nurse says. "That's the NG tube. It's feeding you. Remember?"

12/12/16: Grace was cleared to leave the ICU today! She is in a step-down unit now. Her legs are REALLY hurting her. . . . Please continue to pray that the pain will subside and Grace will regain sufficient strength and alertness to pass the various evaluations from the doctors . . .

My heart breaks to see my sweet wife in this condition, in so much pain, struggling to do so many of the things she once did with ease.

It happens when I least expect it. Sometimes, they catch me off guard as I fall asleep. Other times, they wake me up—as if I wouldn't notice Mom or Ivan rubbing my feet and moving my legs back and forth like a bicycle. They might as well douse me with scalding oil. Nothing makes them feel sorry for me and stop, no matter how much I scream and cry.

12/19/16: Grace is scheduled for the gastrostomy tomorrow, unless she passes the swallow test. Please pray that either way, she will continue to recover in terms of swallowing and, eventually, eating and drinking . . .

In addition, please pray for the next transition coming up in Grace's journey to recovery, the transition to rehabilitation. Please pray that Grace will be approved to go to an acute rehab facility, where she will receive intensive therapy every day, and that, if possible, she will not have to spend time at a skilled nursing facility, where there is a greater chance of poorer conditions and less intensive therapy.

One morning, Mom tells me I've failed all my daily swallow tests. They're going to put a tube in my stomach. The only test I remember is today's, and I don't see how anyone could swallow anything with a camera rammed up their nose and down their throat. But I also hate how the NG tube blisters my throat, and I don't believe it's feeding me, anyway. Maybe a stomach tube means I'll feel full. Maybe I can try eating real food again.

12/23/16: Great news today! A lady from the acute rehab place came and said that Grace is good to go! The last step is a final clearance by the Kaiser doctor in charge of Grace's rehab. Two things need to happen: her white blood cell count needs to go down, and they need to monitor how she responds to her feeding through the stomach tube. So, Grace could be transferred either tomorrow or within the next few days! Please pray that the timing of her transfer will work out smoothly in terms of Grace starting therapy (staff might be thinner on Christmas) and also in terms of insurance coverage (Grace has a limited number of days at acute rehab).

35

December 24th, 2016: Into the Darkness

"Are you sure I'm getting a bath first?" My brain is just alert enough to wonder how often I'll be bathed in the new place.

"Yes, sweetie. The nurse said she'd be here to help in a little bit."

Mom leans over from her chair by my bed and brushes some hair out of my mouth. "What if they come before she gets here?"

"I'll make sure you get your bath. Why don't you get some rest and I'll wake you up when it's closer to time?"

I close my eyes but the pain coursing through my legs won't let me fall asleep.

"Mom?"

"Hmm?"

"I need more pain meds."

"We already went over this, doll." She puts down her sudoku booklet. "You can't go to Casa Colina if you're still on IV narcotics."

"But I need them *now.*"

"They've already given you everything they can today. They're going to unplug you all the way at 5:00 p.m. See, it's almost 2:30." She points to a round mass of gibberish hanging on the wall.

"Mom."

"How about this. I'll run and ask for a basin and cloth, and we'll start your bath early. You'll feel better once you're clean."

I try savoring the warm, soapy water trickling down my scalp and into the yellow bucket behind my head, but the invisible irons searing my legs and left side are too hot.

Later that night, my hair is cold and hard as transporters bump my gurney out the hospital's back door and into the frigid December air. Panic grips my entire body when the ambulance doors close and neither Ivan nor Mom gets in.

"Miss?" A light flickers above my head but I can't see who's talking. "Can you verify your Social Security Number, Miss?"

Social Security Number. My mind sputters hopefully for a few seconds, then burns out. "I don't know what that is."

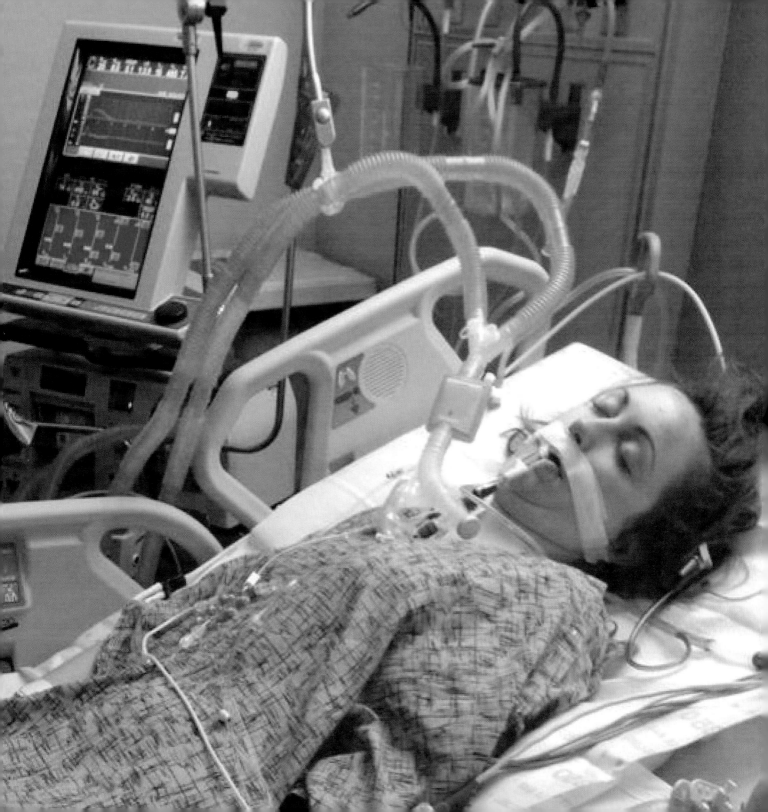

December 30th, 2016: Things Not Seen

"It's your anniversary tomorrow, honey?"

I grimace as the nurse redresses the feeding tube protruding from my stomach.

"Technically, yes."

"Which one?"

"First."

"You look so young. I thought he was your boyfriend!"

I've stopped tallying how often I hear this, but I force a smile.

"How old are you, anyway?"

"Twenty-three."

She clucks and shakes her head.

"I'd ask if you have plans, but I guess we both know the answer to that one."

Ivan is late to dinner that night. He's spent the day moving from our rickety, second-story apartment to a first-floor handicap unit. It must be raining since his coat sprays wet droplets all over my blanket when he slings it over the chair by my bed.

But I notice more cause for concern than a wet jacket, as he gulps down his plate of hospital fried rice. Ivan's eyes are large and rounded in spite of his Asian heritage, so I'm startled by how narrow and strained they seem tonight.

"Hey, Ivan?" It takes me several tries to get his attention, with my voice still gravelly from the respirator, and my roommate enjoying her crime show on the other side of the curtain.

"I'm not mad about all this. Are you? I mean, things could have been so much worse.

They said I should have died that night."

"I know."

Does he think I can't handle the truth?

"But we both believe God has some sort of purpose for keeping me alive, right?" I coax.

"Right." Ivan leans over and kisses me before finishing his rice. I can't stop watching his eyes.

January 17th, 2017: Homeward Bound I

UPDATE #26: *Grace was discharged from Casa Colina yesterday! Praise God.* 🙂 *We spent the night at our friend's house because ADA[1] improvements at our apartment still needed to finish.*

But, as of around noon today, Grace is officially home! 🙂 *Praise God.*

At this point, our apartment is still somewhat of a hospital setting because Grace needs continued medical attention, now administered by me and Grace's mom. We can't wait to visit with everyone freely, but, at this time, it's still important to limit the number of visitors Grace can see due to her brain injury's risk of overstimulation. Thank you all for your understanding, and for your continued support! Your prayers, love, and gifts mean so much to us. We will continue to trust God through this. To Him be the glory!

Part Two

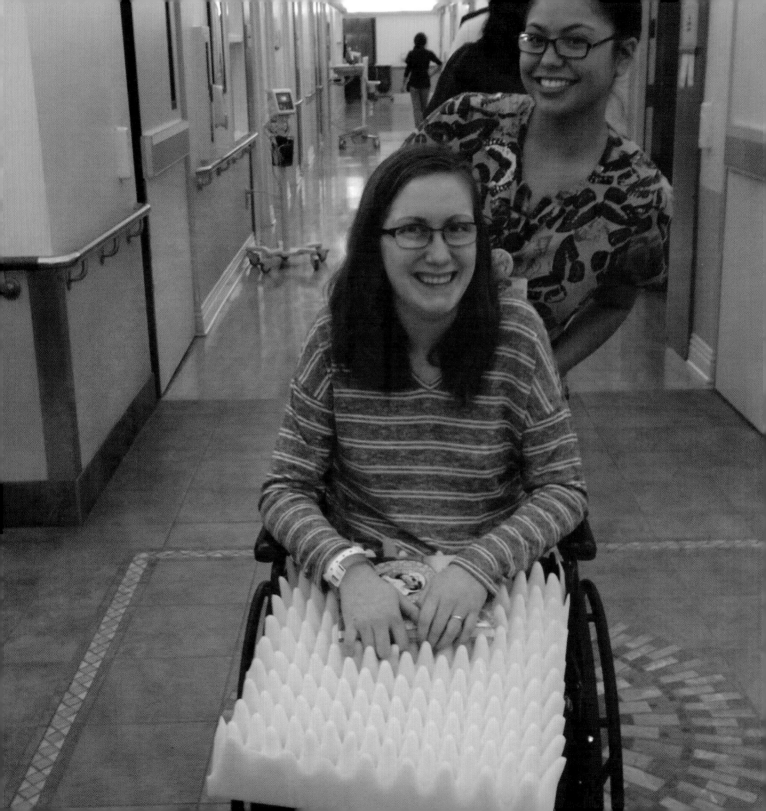

Homeward Bound II

In our picture, my smile is lopsided but happy. My hair's damp from the shower, some novel's balanced on my knee, and brand new loungewear clings to my still-emaciated figure. The CNA is beaming, too, although I'm sure she's posed for countless discharge photos as she escorts patients in their final steps out of Casa Colina.

Even my wheelchair is spotless.

Mom probably took the picture since Ivan would have been retrieving the car. He's the fastest driver, and it's essential to shorten our thirty-minute drive to Chino Hills. The charge nurse told us yesterday that we would need to pick up my discharge meds from our home Kaiser in Riverside, which is thirty minutes in the opposite direction of Chino Hills. My doses come every four hours.

Can't they discharge me with a few doses to tide us over? We're heading to a friend's house in Chino Hills, not our apartment in Riverside, since the apartment's ADA renovations are behind schedule. The nurse had shaken her head sadly. She couldn't change the fact that my rehab contract expires today, or that Casa Colina doesn't hand out narcotics. Our only choice is to pray that Kaiser Riverside fills my prescriptions promptly—and that I survive a night unaccommodated in the guest house Mom and Ivan have slept in during the past three weeks.

I still look happy in that picture. Perhaps I don't realize how easy it is to fall while transferring from a wheelchair to the toilet in a bathroom for able-bodied people. I certainly can't imagine three hours of agony after the Kaiser pharmacy loses my prescriptions.

Maybe it wouldn't have mattered. All those wordless nights pointing at the ICU exit, all those mornings in rehab watching "Xs" march slowly down the January calendar are over. It's January 17th, 2017. I'm homeward bound.

An Additional Comment from Grace

Neurologists warn my family that my brain is too severely injured for anyone to predict my cognitive function when I wake from the coma. Will I be able to think? Converse? Read and write? My mental age is about three years old when I finally open my eyes. By God's grace, I'll recover all the way to thinking like a teenager by the time I'm discharged six weeks later.

I'm not told any of this until months later—until Ivan's sure I can handle the somber, grown-up reality of December 2016. His story may be the complete one, but I'm still most impressed by my own sketchy memories of "growing up" that December: memories of God reintroducing Himself in simple ways that I could understand at the time.

God began with books. Soon after I woke up, someone arranged an inviting stack of books near the left side of my bed, including my Bible, Dickens's *A Christmas Carol* (Ivan and I had been reading that together), and Homer's *Iliad*. (Someone must have known I was hiding that in my desk at work.) I surprised everyone by not asking for any of my books, even though I usually read voraciously. But Ivan persevered in reading the Bible to me every night, whether or not my injured brain could focus on the words.

One morning a nurse came in to change the bag on my IV. She was pushing her big, gray cart as usual, but this time her cart read MEDS on the side, in giant, red letters. It didn't say that before! Or did it? I suppose there had always been letters stenciled on the cart, but they'd looked like nonsense and I was in too much pain to investigate. This morning's discovery snapped me alert and I looked around the rest of my room. Sure enough, the jumbled black and red letters above the door spelled "EXIT." Praise God, I could read again.

Exhausted, my brain drifted off to sleep and I forgot to tell anyone about this miracle for several years.

By the time I was transferred to Casa Colina, a neurological rehab hospital, my reading ability had greatly improved. Unfortunately, my brain still fatigued abnormally quickly. I could barely make it through half a page before my mind wandered off to the twilight zone. Even when Ivan read the Bible to me at night, my attention wavered after about five minutes. But now I was mentally alert enough to suspect there was more to following Christ than reading or listening to the Bible. Was I supposed to pray or something? I drew a blank. I knew what prayer was—visitors and my family prayed over me several times a day. I just couldn't conceive of doing it alone.

"Hello, God," I ventured, a couple of mornings after I'd transferred to Casa Colina. That was it. I didn't know what else to say.

A few days later, I decided to expand my prayer repertoire by copying what other people said when they prayed over me:

"Dear God, thank you for this day . . . this food . . . this visit . . ."

Some of them asked for things as well:

"Please let this appointment go well . . . help the pain to go away . . . let Grace go home soon."

These "asking prayers" satisfied me for a few more weeks. They were the main type of prayer I heard from the people around me and, since Ivan was reading me the Gospel of Matthew, they also seemed like the most common way people prayed to Jesus back in Bible times.

Shortly after I was discharged from the hospital, God restored my mind enough to realize that my "asking prayers" were little more than painting by numbers. It's good to ask for things, but having a meaningful conversation with another person is more than copying others or reciting a list.

What now?

I tried making up a few prayers of my own, but my brain still checked out within seconds of closing my eyes. I'm not sure if someone suggested the idea to me, or if it was God's direct prompting, but one day in early March I remembered the Book of Psalms in the Bible. Weren't psalms supposed to be written prayers to God, arranged as poetry? Surely learning to pray by copying psalms from the Bible wouldn't be quite so "paint by numbers" because each psalm is inspired by God. That makes them perfect models for prayer!

I don't remember what happened next. I wish I remembered my first extemporaneous prayer, or exactly when I resumed a traditional prayer life. My neurological trauma has erased those memories. The important point is that I learned to pray again by studying how the Bible depicts us praying to God. Many of the psalms are distressed, even depressed in character. Some are overwhelmingly joyful. Psalm 119's clear message and intricate stanzas admonished me to treasure the Word of God in and of itself. By God's grace, I can now pray with my eyes closed and for long periods of time. But I don't think anything will replace the sweetness of opening the Scriptures and meditating on a psalm as a prelude for personal prayer.

January 2017: The Journey Begins

The blog is an exit strategy. During my stay in Casa Colina, I'd been horrified when Ivan revealed his daily Facebook updates with their dozens of shares and hundreds of likes.

"But I don't know that many people!" I protest.

"Our families work with churches in the US and Asia," he reminds me gently.

Ivan doesn't show me the original updates since I've always hated attracting attention. I also don't tell him to stop posting. If God is using my story to encourage people, so be it.

"What are you guys going to do about Facebook?" Mom asks over our second or third meal at home. She's putting the finishing touches on some mashed potatoes.

"Facebook?" Ivan is eating and helping me navigate my own plate at the same time. As much progress as I made in rehab, I still struggle to swallow some foods—and eat without using my left hand.

"It does seem like people still want updates." I had forced myself to read Ivan's last couple of posts. "But it's kind of weird for Ivan to keep writing now I'm home."

"*You* could use Facebook." He passes me a tiny piece of braised broccoli.

I look at the broccoli dubiously.

I'm just not a Facebook person. There's got to be a better way."

The better way is probably Mom's idea. She's still hovering by the stove, perhaps fussing over the potatoes as she did when I was little, or giving us an extra moment alone as she will for the next five months. *What about a blog*? It sounds like a good compromise since I don't believe it will last long now I'm home. Bowing out of a private blog is a lot less embarrassing than watching Facebook "likes" evaporate.

"What do y'all think we should call it? If we're going to do this, it should at least sound catchy." I'm typing random names into my new WordPress account.

"What about 'Walking with Grace'?" Mom is scrubbing a skillet with steel wool. "After all, our biggest question is: when will you start walking again?"

I consider. "Walking with Grace" has a ring to it.

"I think you might be onto something. Sayang?"[2] I try using Indonesian since Ivan's buried in his laptop. "What do you think about 'Walking with Grace'?"

"Walking with what?" He looks from me to Mom blankly. "*Walking with Grace*. For the blog."

"Oh. Yeah, that could work."

I punch it in, skeptical that no bloggers have walked gracefully before me.

"Walking with Grace" available. Click here *to claim.*

I click.

February 2017: A Journal for Your Thoughts

Ivan's journal is my favorite shade of caramel. Fleur-de-lis score its buttery leather spine, and Jeremiah 29:11 flows across the cover:

> "For I know The Plans
>
> I HAVE FOR YOU
>
> Declares the LORD
>
> TO PROSPER YOU
>
> And not to Harm You
>
> Plans to Give You HOPE &
>
> A FUTURE."

But Ivan doesn't buy journals and he's definitely not a hipster. In late November, an eccentric mother had presented it in lieu of a tip for performing at her daughter's voice recital. Ivan was too nice to request a standard tip, and I was too amused to complain.

"At least you have a new hobby," I'd joked.

I rediscover Ivan's journal in mid-February while scrounging for scratch paper—perhaps for an occupational therapy drill—and ask Ivan about it that night after dinner.

"Hey, Sayang?"

"Mmm?" He's already landed on the couch and opened his laptop. Between homework and job applications, Ivan's glued to his laptop almost every minute he's at home.

"Isn't this the journal you got right before . . . before the accident?"

"The what?" He peers at the brown object in my hand.

"You know, the journal." I raise my voice over Mom washing dishes in the kitchen. "From the *recital*?"

"Oh, that journal." His fingers fly across the laptop keyboard. "Do you think you're going to use it?"

"Maybe. I dunno."

I look down at my wheelchair. The left wheel has something stuck to it even though Mom's already wiped both wheels twice today. It's two months after the accident but I still hate asking people to help me.

"Cuz I'll take it if you won't."

"You're going to start journaling?" Ivan stops typing and looks over at me.

So he does remember I hate asking for things, at least, his things.

"You don't seem like much of a journaler."

"I *can* try something new. But don't let me take it away from you."

"Sure, go ahead. I'd forgotten I had it anyway."

Mom drops a pot in the kitchen and we both flinch.

Ivan resumes typing and I relax my grip on the journal, relieved that my nails haven't left permanent marks in the synthetic leather. Something about his face seems jaded, a shadow of the new husband who used to dump his backpack under the keyboard and watch movies with me at night, or take me out for yogurt when a student canceled, or even just look me in the eye when I asked a question.

"Okay, but only if you're sure." Ivan's already too busy to hear, but I still say it to make someone feel better, perhaps Mom, probably just me.

You don't seem like much of a journaler. His comment is more true than I'll admit. I've tried keeping journals ever since I was nine years old, but it never stuck. Perhaps I try again simply out of boredom. What else can I do in a three-room apartment when my brain is still too fragile for visitors? Or perhaps I try because part of me already knows that writing will become my life.

This time the habit sticks. At first, my entries are short and simple, but they develop quickly as my brain heals and my activities broaden. Within a few months, I am spending at least thirty minutes a day recording the minutiae of my physical, mental, and emotional experiences. The only blank pages are on days I write blog posts, and eventually I'll even mark those spaces as blog days so I have an excuse for not writing. Perhaps people naturally believe that someone will read their journal one day.

From Ivan and Grace

Grace: During that first critical month at home, I didn't have much time to consider who might read my journal. Ivan and I could barely keep ourselves afloat from one day to the next.

I've been the consummate overachiever ever since high school. (How many teens practice violin four hours a day while working part time at the county zoo and teaching violin lessons, all to prepare and save for college?) These tendencies carried me through undergrad and even began martialing our fledgling marriage. As a new wife, I'd rise before my alarm every morning at 6:00 a.m., dress my corporate best for my day job at Ivan's university, then dash to the kitchen. One breakfast bowl and two lunch sacks later, I'd fly back to the bedroom to grab high heels and yank the covers off my sleep-ridden husband.

"You're going to be late for school if you don't get up right now!" I'd bark.

Having washed my hands of his (mis)fortune, I'd grab myself a pop tart and the lunch bag with the hummus wrap, then sally forth into the blinding sunlight—all in time to clock in outside my office at 7:30 a.m. sharp.

Back then, I'd been a Monarch butterfly, vibrant with possibility. Now I'm a misshapen caterpillar—too blind to imagine a cocoon.

Now Ivan lifts me from my wheelchair into bed every night. I'm not allowed to put any weight on my legs, so the "extra high" queen bed we'd snagged from IKEA for its spacious storage drawers is no longer such a great deal. But transferring into bed is only the beginning of our nightly routine. Although Mom's graciously offered to stay in Riverside and help care for me until Ivan graduates in May, there is one task she cannot stomach: wound care.

Every evening, Ivan lifts me carefully into bed and lowers me onto my back, then raises my shirt to expose the feeding tube that was placed in my stomach last December. We found out it had been placed incorrectly a couple of weeks after the surgery when the orifice around the tube developed a nasty infection and an angry constellation of pressure sores. But the surgeon has insisted we leave the tube in place until my stomach heals from the original procedure. Until then, Ivan must sponge away its repulsive discharge every morning and evening, baste the sores with lidocaine, and manage my antibiotics' taper schedule.

When I heard the surgeon's treatment plan, I was terrified. Ivan can't get himself out of bed on time. How can he possibly be trusted with a regimen like this?

But Ivan never misses a round of wound care. He rises promptly at 6:00 a.m., disposes of the wrappers from my 2:00 a.m. narcotics dose, then returns to my side of the bed. More often than not, he's carrying my favorite blanket, a plush, crimson and cream lap robe that some anonymous benefactor must have left for me at Casa Colina. Ivan understands these February mornings are nightmarish: shivering grinds my broken bones together mercilessly, and the piercing, pre-dawn chill freezes the titanium hardware inside my legs.

"You know we've gotta do this, Sayang." Ivan will venture, then pass me the blanket as a peace offering.

"It'll only take a minute!" He lifts my night shirt.

I close my eyes and grit my teeth, cursing his probing, frozen fingers.

"All over now!" Ivan's learned to clean the tube and paint the sores in less than two minutes. Now he's raising me gently to a seated position. Sitting up requires abdominal strength, and my belly is compromised.

"Let's get you in your chair!" Ivan places me on the eggshell cushion in my wheelchair and wraps me in my favored blanket until I feel like I've been swallowed by a fleecy, red cocoon. He grabs another blanket from his side of the bed and throws it across my knees for good measure.

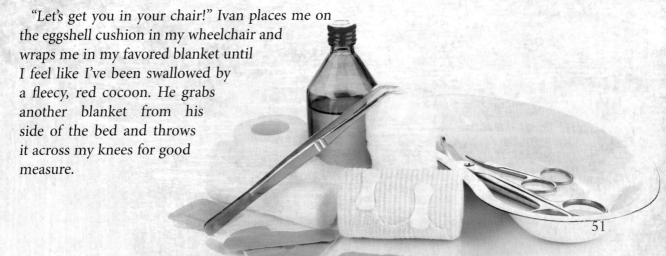

"Look who we have here!" Ivan muscles open our bedroom door and rolls me into the kitchen triumphantly. Mom is pouring three bowls of cereal.

"Oh—sorry Mom, but I'd better shower before I head for school."

"You have to eat something." Mom's maternal indignation is less persuasive before she's had coffee.

"Don't worry! I'll grab a pop tart on the way out." Ivan heads back to the bedroom to grab his clothes, then makes a break for the bathroom.

"When does school start, anyway?"

"7:30" Ivan shouts from the bathroom, keeping perfect time with my answer.

"He'd better hurry or he's going to be late," Mom observes to no one in particular.

"Don't worry." I smile. "Ivan's got everything under control."

❖

Ivan: Grace and I were thrust into new roles the moment the Mercedes shattered her body. I was now a caregiver for my wife. I processed this metamorphosis clinically, calculating how to respond. I did not even panic the night of the accident when doctors told me that Grace had suffered two strokes and had been put in a medically induced coma. God was stretching me to my limits in this new role—perhaps beyond them.

Those first months of recovery felt like whitewater rafting, continuously navigating rocks and rapids and half expecting to be dashed to pieces any minute. The

stream of legal responsibilities, medical developments, and last-minute emergencies was endless. I did not allow myself to process any of my emotions deeply for two reasons: first, I feared what I'd find if I truly looked inside myself; second, I simply had no time.

In the early days after Grace's discharge, my mornings began by helping her get dressed and into her wheelchair. I'm surprised at how quickly I adjusted to wheeling Grace around our small apartment. Memories of us walking together grew distant, almost like clips from a previous life.

Grace's mom lived with us for the first five months after the accident so I could leave Grace at home while I worked and went to class. That spring was my last semester of grad school. I'd been studying piano performance and music composition for the past two years. Now that Grace was disabled, I was also working four part-time jobs to make ends meet and replace her lost income. Depending on the day of the week (or time of day), I was a private piano teacher, a high school choir pianist, a church pianist, or a freelance musician. Our medical insurance still came through Grace's full-time job at my university; now that she was on disability, we had only six more months of coverage before that insurance ran out.

In the meantime, my days were filled with caretaking, school, work, and applications for full-time jobs. Caretaking included everything from managing wound care to administering blood-thinner injections, and from helping Grace shower and dress to coaching her as she ate. (Due to the strokes, her right hand was functional but her left hand was not.) Both her mom and I helped her practice physical and occupational therapy exercises every day. Our household withstood these immense pressures only by God's grace. His grace could take the form of anything from a meal delivered by a friend to encouraging prayers, cards, and texts, and even to gentle reminders that nothing escapes God's watchful, tender providence.

Everyone's life depends on God's providence—it's just that some of us won't admit it until we're pushed beyond our limits. God used Grace's acute recovery to show me that He is more than able to help His children persevere through unforeseeable troubles. Apart from God, I would have capsized under the rigorous hardships we were facing. I was a little raft caught up in a raging river; God was the pilot who guided me to safety.

February 11th, 2017: "But Even if Not . . ."

"Yesterday was my second orthopedic follow-up at Kaiser after the initial surgeries in December. I was so excited! I hadn't yet been allowed to put any weight on my legs, but I was sure yesterday that I'd get the green light to begin learning to walk. I wasn't even nervous before the appointment because I was so confident about how things would turn out.

We began my follow-up in Radiology, a dark cluster of rooms in the hospital's basement.

I executed some painful contortions so the tech could photograph my healing tibias. Then we headed to Orthopedics on the third floor. We were shown to an exam room almost immediately, and I couldn't wait to receive the joyous prognosis after the physician assistant reviewed my x-rays.

"So far it looks like you're healing well," he turned from the computer monitor and smiled. I returned his smile and began an internal happy dance. "I think we can give it one more month and then you can begin putting weight on your legs."

My happy dance ended abruptly. I managed a neutral "Oh, okay," trying not to look crestfallen. Both Ivan and I were tongue-tied, but Mom remained sharp enough to ask for an adjusted timetable. "Progressing from weight-bearing to walking couldn't be that hard, right?"

"Six months to a year to learn to walk, and one to two years to be able to walk well," he answered.

I haven't made peace with yesterday's news, and we haven't figured out what our lives will look like for the next year. But I also can't stop thinking of the Bible story about Shadrach, Meshach, and Abednego. Although it's too long to share here, the short version of it is that the king of Babylon threatened to throw these three men into a furnace unless they stopped worshiping God and started worshiping the king. Their answer always amazes me:

"If the God we serve exists, then He can rescue us from the furnace of blazing fire, and He can rescue us from the power of you, the king. *But even if He does not rescue us*, we want you as king to know that we will not serve your gods or worship the gold statue you set up" (Dan. 3:17-18, CSB, italics mine).

Their response is where I am at right now. I know that God is able to heal me, and I do believe I'll learn to walk—even walk *well*—one day. But if He takes longer, or chooses not to heal me at all, God is still God, and, absolutely, He's still good."

The post seems formulaic at best: tie devastating news to an inspirational Bible story, admit *some* discomfort—not enough to make anyone feel awkward—then end with a smile and a prayer. Some savvy readers might suspect they're reading a story retouched for social media filter. No one could react that positively to learning they'd spend several more months in a wheelchair.

But those readers would be mistaken. I did write exactly what I thought and felt that day. Perhaps my brain had adjusted to bad news being possible, even probable. (There's not much worse than waking up to be told you've been hit by a car.) Or perhaps I was still "growing up" as I healed from the brain injury, and so couldn't take the news as seriously as a healthy adult.

I believe the most likely explanation for my response was that God protected me from those traumatic, occasionally sinful emotions we often associate with dramatic suffering and loss. In the Bible story I shared, we don't read about Shadrach, Meshach, and Abednego developing PTSD around fires after God rescued them from the furnace. We also don't find anything about them displaying chronic rage or toxic bitterness toward their fellow courtiers, even though it's likely our three survivors would have faced objects, people, and situations that reminded them of their near-death experience every day.

No. When God redeems His children, He redeems every part of them: mind, body, and spirit. He may leave some parts of us outwardly broken for reasons we don't understand, but there's no disability, trauma, or even everyday stressor that He can't choose to heal at a moment's notice. Every part of our lives as believers has been set apart, an instrument for His glory. Whether or not God resolves a specific trial, we must join with Shadrach, Meshach, and Abednego in praising God's power and trusting His plan.

February 28th, 2017 . . . He is Still Good

"One, two, three—go!" The harness begins lifting my bottom upward, gently but forcefully upward. I don't know whether to follow my instincts to lean back and resist or to push down with my legs and help the machine to do its work.

"There you go, Grace," my therapist coaxes. "Just a little bit more. Just a little bit . . . " Suddenly, I'm standing on my own two feet.

I hold my breath for the stabs of excruciating pain I'm expecting after three months of jaw-clenching therapy. Nothing comes. I wobble peacefully atop the two tree trunks that used to be my legs.

Was I ever this tall?

I survey the therapists, patients, and exercise machines that usually dwarf my wheelchair. Many of them are shorter than I am! I've felt subhuman ever since I woke from the coma, but I never imagined it was because my eyes were level with the average person's bottom.

"Grace?" My therapist's voice slices into my thoughts. "That's five minutes."

"Five minutes? Already?"

Mom is beaming as she swipes through photos on her phone.

"You got *pictures*?"

She nods.

"How do I get . . ." My heart begins to race: I can't tolerate the notion of sitting down by myself. A sharp pain flashes through my left knee.

"Relax, honey." My therapist punches a button. "The machine's got you."

I go limp as the harness lowers me to my original seated position in the wheelchair. All my muscles are quivering like Jell-o. Everyone holds their breath to see what I'll say.

"I did it!" Somehow laughing feels appropriate.

"I got some great pictures for Ivan," Mom points to her phone.

That takes the wind out of my sails a bit.

"I wish he wasn't working all the time." I pick at some loose threads on my legging. The sick pay from my full-time job will run out next week, so Ivan has started working sixty hours a week to get a head start on rent and groceries.

"But you stood in February, ten days earlier than your orthopedic doctor predicted."

"I always say doctors are too cautious," my therapist comments proudly. "You looked more than ready to me, so I didn't see why we should wait for a specific date."

I smile, grateful that my therapist ignored those negative predictions even when I didn't.

What did Jesus see, looking down at us—me, Mom, and Ivan—that momentous afternoon? We were harried by the daily chaos of staying out of the ER, keeping up in therapy, and running our tiny, one-bedroom apartment like a rehab hospital. Constant little crises (like running out of specifically sized gauze squares, for which we could not substitute our other gauze squares, because the missing ones needed to be *folded and then cut in half* to be the right size for my pressure sores) convinced us we had no time to stop for a routine family prayer time, much less take an actual day of rest.

I imagine Jesus looking down at us, that day I stood for the first time, something like how he'd looked at his disciples the night they insisted they were about to be shipwrecked and drowned in the Sea of Galilee:

"And they went and woke him, saying, 'Save us, Lord; we are perishing.' And he said to them, 'Why are you afraid, O you of little faith?' Then he rose and rebuked the winds and the sea, and there was a great calm" (Matt. 8:25-26).

God knew He was going to heal me ahead of the doctor's schedule. I'll always wonder how much more peaceful those last weeks of waiting might have been if I'd admitted my vision of God's calendar was only human—and very imperfect.

Walking with Grace

My brain is relearning which memories to file and which to discard. I'll realize this when I discover that what should be a climax—taking my first steps—only exists as a journal entry. No matter what I try, that moment remains locked inside a short paragraph:

March 6th, 2017: *I walked today! Wow. Definitely did not know that was going to happen when I woke up this morning. I thought today would be a follow-up to the standing practice I did last week, so I was super surprised when they told me I'd been transferred from Liz, the therapy assistant who's worked with me for my whole time at Kaiser, to Pam, the head therapist. I was even more surprised when Pam pulled out a walker and gave me instructions for taking my first steps! It went surprisingly well, with minimal pain and wobbling, and I even made one lap across the gym! Not only that, but I'm cleared to walk short distances on the walker at home!! This is all way ahead of schedule, and I couldn't be more thankful to the Lord for the best pre-birthday present ever!!!*

What did Ivan say when he got home? Did Mom show him a video of my first steps?

What was it like puttering around our apartment those first few days? One day I'll forgive myself for not knowing.

Ivan's Thoughts

One of the first medical phrases I learned after Grace's accident was "bilateral tibial plateau fracture." In other words, Grace broke both her knees right under the kneecap, on top of the tibia. She also damaged arteries in her left leg and foot. These injuries meant Grace needed eight hours of back-to-back orthopedic and vascular surgeries to repair her legs. The procedures took place while she was still in a coma, about a week after the accident.

Thank God, the surgeries went well. The orthopedic surgeon later explained that if the fractures had occurred just a few inches higher, Grace might have never walked again. Inches matter to God.

For the next three months, Grace was not allowed to put any weight or pressure on her legs. Not that she wanted to—her legs were hurting both from the fractures as well as from the severe neuropathy, or nerve pain, left over from her two strokes.

Somehow Grace survived all the pain and proceeded to her next phase of relearning to walk, intensive physical therapy. She worked so hard, focusing all her willpower on doing whatever she had to do to get better. I was overjoyed when I heard she stood for the very first time in her therapy class. I had just come home from work, and Grace and her mom looked as though they could barely contain themselves with their remarkably good news. Grace's accomplishment seemed like a miracle to us.

When I'd imagined being married, I never dreamed of helping my wife relearn how to walk. Yet that was my passion in

Spring 2017. After Grace had been given a walker, she and I spent Saturday afternoons outdoors either in the church parking lot to the left of our apartment complex, or in the university parking lot to its right. These were short forays, but even small, slow steps were a marathon that required training. Grace was a dedicated athlete, willing her legs to function despite pain and fatigue. I remember one occasion, maybe more, when her legs gave out before we completed our loop, and I had to carry her home.

God was still good even if Grace's progress seemed slow. Eventually, she would build enough strength and stamina in her legs to walk independently almost all the time. Six years after the accident, she doesn't limp unless she's fatigued.

How much does Grace's journey to walking again resemble our spiritual walk with the Lord? Just as I helped Grace while she learned to stand, take baby steps, then walk, how often does God patiently pick us up when we've collapsed under our sins? Do we realize how often God infuses us with His strength, empowering us to take the next step? Have we truly thanked Him for never leaving us nor giving up on us? How lovingly God carries us when we're too broken to stand at all!

If life is a journey, what is our destination? Are we pressing on "toward the goal for the prize of the upward call of God in Christ Jesus?" (Phil. 3:14). Or are we walking in endless, self-oriented circles that eventually lead away from God?

Lord, give us Your grace to walk humbly and faithfully with You.

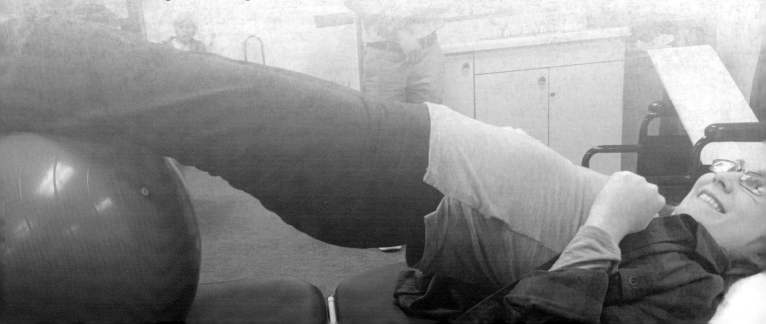

The Silence of Music

Learning to walk isn't the only memory my brain files incorrectly. I barely remember repairing my violin in Los Angeles, even though my journal reveals that day as transformative. Why does my brain delete the memories that matter most?

March 9th, 2017: Yesterday was a big day! A pipe broke somewhere in our apartment complex around 6:00 a.m. and maintenance decided they needed to turn off everyone's water for most of the day. We needed to spend the day somewhere for bathroom/eating purposes, so Mom suggested heading to LA to pick up my violin from the luthier. I did much better handling the ninety-minute drive and my anxiety, but the real stunner came in the luthier's shop. When he handed me my violin and bow, I could tell by the look in his eyes that he wanted me to do more than admire his work—he wanted me to play. (He knew my accident story; also, he sold me my first full-sized violin when I was ten.) My heart started pounding since I knew from previous failed attempts that my left hand couldn't work like that yet. But something in his expression made me want to try again. This time my fingers found a one-octave G Major scale! The notes were very wobbly and very slow, but they were still real notes! I couldn't believe I did it, and neither could Ivan, Mom, or the luthier. I think this is a sign God is going to give the violin back to me, and also a reminder that when He does, that's what I'm supposed to do with my life.

I didn't post this story on the blog. In fact, I wouldn't refer to the violin for another fifty-one weeks.

"Why get everyone's hopes up?" I hedge when Ivan asks about my silence. It's painful enough responding to prying texts, and fringe research articles, and stories of miraculously healed third cousins. Imagine what would happen if I revealed that I'd actually made a little progress?

What I really mean is, *Why get* my *hopes up?* I claim to believe in miracles—I even said so in my journal—but some part of me can't risk the agony of disappointment. After all, God didn't heal everyone in the Bible. What if He doesn't heal me?

A Different Kind of Harmony

From Ivan and Grace

Grace: My violin journey begins—humanly speaking—almost randomly. When I was five years old, my family moved from Asheville, NC, to Los Angeles, CA, so my father could attend seminary. I turned six before the following school year, but my parents were uncomfortable about sending me to school alone in our disreputable district. Instead, they decided to homeschool me, and eventually my younger sister, Anna.

At that time in California, "homeschooling" meant registering with a charter school for academic supervision. This regulation turned into a blessing for our family: Mom did her research well and selected a charter that sponsored field trips to survival hikes, Shakespeare workshops, famous museums like the Getty and Huntington Gardens, and even . . . Disneyland. In addition to these big-ticket field trips, the charter also sponsored one semester of arts classes at a community school high in the misty hills of La Cañada, tucked well away from our asphalt-melting Los Angeles heat.

One afternoon at the beginning of first grade, Mom interrupted my playtime to ask a serious question. I was rolling around on our bedroom floor, tussling with Charles, our Siamese cat. It was still blazing hot in the San Fernando Valley, so Anna and I hadn't been outside in ages. Recently, Mom had taken to closing blinds as yet another feeble defense against the heat. She spent many afternoons in our darkened "children's room," puzzling over an intricate jigsaw of the Rosetta Stone.

"Grace, I keep forgetting to ask you. Would you like to take art lessons? For fun?"

"Isn't that what we did with Miss Rhonda last year?" I went back to playing with my cat.

"Yes, but this is different. This time you get to go for an entire class. Like, a *school* class." She knitted her eyebrows in consternation as she continued testing spots for her puzzle piece. "But you don't have to do art if you don't want to. The brochure said you could pick art, ballet, or violin."

"Violin. Definitely." I kissed the top of Charles's head, smoothing his glossy fur down his spine all the way to his tail. I had no idea what a violin was.

The group class didn't last long. The instructor noticed I learned quickly and had an unusually good ear, and strongly recommended to my parents that they enroll me in private lessons. But my dad was a student and my mom was a homemaker. Violin was all well and good while the state paid for it. The state, however, did not sponsor private music lessons. Where was this tuition supposed to come from? By God's grace, my parents enrolled me in private violin lessons anyway. I was too young to wonder, much less understand, how they worked it out. All I knew was that I now had a violin lesson every Tuesday afternoon *all by myself.* I could learn songs as fast as I wanted—no need to wait for other students to catch up. And the pieces got harder and harder. They began having funny, foreign-sounding names like "étude" and "concerto."

Like many gifted children, I had the privilege of studying with several teachers during my childhood and teenage years. My parents and I switched once out of necessity, when my dad graduated from seminary in Los Angeles and we moved to his first church in Green Bay, Wisconsin. Other times, my parents transitioned me to work on a specific technique with someone known for teaching it, or to get a fresh set of eyes when I got too comfortable with how I sounded.

The world of young classical musicians is very similar to that of high school athletes. There are more "gifted" teenagers than there are seats in youth orchestras, parts in chamber ensembles, competitions to win, scholarships to score—not to mention college auditions. The school on a graduate's diploma—more specifically, the student's professor at that school—often influences the student's success as he or she tries breaking into the saturated, preexisting world of professional musicians. To a teen with her heart set on becoming the first violin of a string quartet sophisticated enough to travel the world, every note counts every time.

In my case, I didn't fully comprehend the implications of *studying* violin until seventh grade. My violin teacher and I were discussing potential repertoire for upcoming competitions. I'd won my divisions the year before, so I was not really worried about the next few months.

"What about this?" To my dismay, Yuliya was holding up Fritz Kreisler's *Rondo,* a famously tricky show piece the virtuoso had transcribed for violin from one of Mozart's serenades. I'd played this piece before so I knew it showcased my flaws: a stiff right bowing arm and left hand fingers that outran the beat.

"*Rondo.* Well, I never thought of picking that one but I guess . . ."

"How much you practicing right now?" Yuliya's Ukrainian accent transforms g's to k's.

"Two hours. Ish."

"And you what, twelve, thirteen years old? I tell you what, in Russia, by the time I was your age, we were practicing three or four hours a day."

Mom gasps from her chair by the door. She sits in all my lessons, taking notes.

"I'm not kidding you. When they took us from home to conservatory, that was what you did if you were going to be violinist." Yuliya scrutinizes my face. "You really wanna be violinist?"

I nod slowly.

"Then here's what's will happen. You gonna start practicing four hours a day: one hour scales, one hour études, two hours concerto and show piece. All right? Because that's what it takes to be good at violin. It's just kids here," she rolls her eyes. "They don't wanna do it. You think you can handle?"

I looked back at Mom, wondering if I would get in trouble for saying yes. I would be, for all intents and purposes, signing my twelve-year-old recreational life away. But Mom smiled encouragingly. I turned back to Yuliya.

"Yeah. I wanna be a violinist."

By my senior year in high school, my days revolved—quite literally—around violin. I got up, ate breakfast, practiced from 8:00 a.m. to 10:00 a.m. Took a break to watch school lectures and work on assignments until lunch at 12:00 p.m. 12:30 p.m. was time to rehearse whichever concerto I was learning at the moment, with Mom playing the orchestral accompaniment on our well-tempered Baldwin grand piano.

Advanced instrumental music students typically study *concerti*, three-movement, virtuosic solos that are intended to be accompanied by an orchestra. Many parents hire pianists to accompany their children, but that was financially out of the question for us. Instead, Mom dusted off what she remembered from her own childhood piano lessons and set to work learning an endless stream of scores by Mozart, Tchaikovsky, Saint-Saëns, and Sibelius.

After rehearsal, I continued practicing my solo repertoire from 1:00 p.m. to 3:00 p.m., then finished my school lectures and took a walk if I had extra time before dinner. Evenings were for finishing homework, and maybe some TV but definitely a novel. Lights out at 10:00 p.m., and repeat. Once I turned sixteen, weekends were for working. Conservatory is frighteningly expensive, and who knew how much financial aid I'd be offered?

One frigid morning in January 2011, I rose before dawn to perform a couple of spots on Green Bay's 5:00 a.m. daily news. I'd won a regional concerto competition a few months earlier, and part of my duties included advertising the upcoming symphony concert where I'd perform as a soloist.

Perhaps that early news spot was a blessing in disguise: I was too sleepy to think about what lay ahead of me, much less feel anything.

The minute my camera's red light stopped flashing, I scurried off the green screen, passed Mom my violin, and sprinted toward our family's formerly white Ford Taurus. *You should've known TV spots would take longer than expected*, I chided myself. *At least Mom drove separately.* The January sun was probably breathtaking as usual, rising across the virgin white farmland, but my eyes were locked on the salty, two-lane Wisconsin highway in front of me. Did I dare break the speed limit?

Somehow, I shimmied into my khaki uniform and clocked in to Guest Services at the Northeast Wisconsin Zoo at 6:58 a.m. The shift manager tossed me a rag and gestured to a bucket of steaming suds.

" 'S gonna be slow up here today. Why don't cha head down to the cafeteria and start scrubbing the underside of them tables. Gives me the creeps."

No comment on my fancy hair and makeup.

Think how much more you'll appreciate the opportunity, I cajoled myself as I kneeled on the soiled cafeteria floor. *Those kids who get their educations handed to them; they have no clue the value they're getting.* I still couldn't keep myself from wondering about the elderly folk who actually got up at 5:00 a.m. to watch the news or the business professionals who donated large sums so the orchestra that was going to accompany my solo could exist. What if they saw me now, on hands and knees, scrubbing unidentifiable substances off a zoo cafeteria table? I burst out laughing. Even I couldn't take myself that seriously.

❖

Ivan: My parents didn't just give me piano lessons growing up. They also taught me what to look for in a future spouse once I was old enough to date. Dating should be intentional, they explained. It wasn't meant to be a low-commitment ticket to round out weekends. From this perspective, the day Grace transferred from the Eastman School of Music in Rochester, NY, to California Baptist University in Riverside, CA, was a momentous one for me.

Grace transferred the junior year of my undergraduate degree, while I was the pianist for the school's University Choir and Orchestra. One afternoon just after Christmas break, our director paused during rehearsal to introduce a new student: a tall, slender girl with long brown hair.

"This is Grace Crosby; she just transferred here from the Eastman School of Music," he announced.

My first reaction was a mix of awe and confusion. Awe, because Eastman was one of the top music schools in the country; confusion, because *Why on earth would a music student transfer from there to a regional, private Christian school?* Surely not for an upgrade in her music education.

Mercifully, the director asked Grace my unspoken question a few seconds later:

"So, Grace, why did you decide to leave Eastman?"

"Well, I really appreciated going there and learning from some of the top teachers in the world; but the environment was very ungodly and self-centered. The emphasis was on promoting yourself, at the expense of others. I knew God didn't want me to stay there."

Wow. Just wow. This was someone I had to meet.

Notwithstanding my natural introversion, I took the first chance I could to introduce myself to Grace. I noticed her kind smile and sharp, thoughtful eyes. The more we talked, the more we discovered all our shared interests: music, of course, but also Tolkien and Lewis, and art, history, literature, philosophy. We clicked.

We didn't start dating officially until about a year after Grace arrived at CBU. We got engaged a year after that, then married six months later on December 30, 2015. By that time, I was a graduate student, and one of our sources of income came from gigs. I played for weddings, memorial services, private parties, theatre shows, and all sorts of other events. Grace also took gigs and taught a couple of students, in addition to working full time as an administrative assistant at CBU. But no matter the occasion, we resoundingly preferred joint gigs where I played piano and she played violin.

For me and Grace, music was more than an activity, more than a profession. It was part of our identity. We affirmed that God would always be our foundation, and our faith would influence every aspect of our lives, including music. But on a human level, for better or worse, music was the air we breathed, the food and water we consumed. Both of us discovered music during childhood; both of us dedicated hours upon hours to lessons, practicing, and performing; now both of us were looking forward to a lifetime of bliss as a violin-piano duo.

This was not to be.

When God sovereignly allowed Grace's accident, He took away her violin-playing via her two strokes. As a pianist and fledgling composer, I had assumed I would write many pieces for violin and piano, and that Grace and I would perform them together. I'd assumed I would always be surrounded by the rich, soaring melodies of her violin, a sonic expression of her inner world, her passion, her creative beauty.

For Grace, losing violin must have been like losing part of herself. For me, it was like losing part of my wife and best friend, losing a lifelong dream.

People respond to loss in different ways. I felt numb. I processed losing Grace's violin-playing in the same clinical way I processed her other medical complications: I focused on accomplishing tasks to keep our family going, to make sure we didn't founder. When something is irreversible, why waste energy trying to reverse it?

I can only imagine how losing her violin actually felt for Grace. It must have devastated her. We didn't talk about the instrument for months, other than to remark on its miraculous survival of the car's initial impact.

As brutal as it was to lose my wife's violin, I gradually realized that *I still had my wife*. Though we will never again perform as a violin-piano duo the way I had imagined, we are still husband and wife, best friends for life. Grace is still Grace. It's as if a forest fire has devastated a region, but the roots of the burned trees are still strong, and new life will come from the ashes.

No accident could take away Grace's love for music: we still attend live performances together and our relationship with music will always be one of love, even if tainted by loss. I can't imagine how wonderful it will be when God restores all things in heaven, where Grace will play her violin again, and I will play alongside her on the piano.

March-May 2017: Who's on First?

The discrepancy between journal entries and blog posts widens with time. Relaying recovery milestones to my Blogging Family is cathartic, while depicting daily TBI[3] dysfunction seems humiliating. What will readers think if they know I panicked in Lululemon, overwhelmed by that lady who leaned over my wheelchair to grab the striped "80 percent off" tank?

I can't tell.

At the end of March, Mom suggests we give readers some explanation of my TBI anxiety. "Why else are you evading visitors when Grace sounds so articulate online?" she asks. I know she's right, but that doesn't calm my nerves. Ivan breaks the stalemate with a tactful coda to his post commemorating four months since the accident:

> *Ivan: "Grace's brain still prevents her from spending time in public places like church, the grocery store, or restaurants. Too much sensory input or overstimulation, such as interacting with multiple people at once, hearing a lot of background noise, or even facing open-ended situations can trigger mild to severe panic attacks. She often loses the ability to speak or even think in these episodes. Doctors say TBI recovery can take months, or years . . . but we'll keep trusting God to lead us one step at a time!"*

"I still have plenty of time," I tell myself as I inhale for a count of four. Mom's just rolled me out of another sparsely populated clothing store. My goal was to stay inside for twenty minutes but I only lasted ten. "Marcia says the brain makes most of its recovery in the first six months, and I still have two to go." Marcia is the neurological occupational therapist who took over my case shortly after I stood. She sounds optimistic.

True to Marcia's prediction, my anxiety stabilizes enough over the next couple of months to see some friends. However, my brain is too cloudy as a result of healing from injuries and narcotic withdrawal to capture more than a few details:

- A friend from work brings over my favorite shrimp pho while I'm still in my wheelchair. I don't know how I eat a dish that requires chopsticks and a spoon since I can only use my right hand.
- One of my bridesmaids probably drops by several times since she lives down the street, but I only have a single memory of her sitting on our shabby velour couch.
- My youngest violin student visits after I learn to walk. I'm glad to see her and apologize for canceling her Christmas recital.
- My college mentor drops by several times as a follow-up to his Casa Colina visits.

I know there are others who drop off food or stay the afternoon, but they hover like ghosts, barely visible if my mind squints just right. We have yet to learn my brain isn't healing as fast as was hoped.

March 23rd, 2017: The Story of an EEG

What in the world is an EEG? And why did I just have one? According to Google, EEG stands for "electroencephalogram." It's a machine that diagnoses brain conditions such as seizures.

Ivan's last blog post mentioned that I had been dealing with anxiety symptoms. Since traumatic brain injuries and strokes can cause anxiety disorders, and since I'd had a brain injury and two strokes, my odds of experiencing anxiety were high. But my anxiety episodes are triggered by different incidents from what you might expect. Most of them happen when my brain gets overstimulated, such as when I'm in a loud or crowded space for too long. When that happens, my brain short circuits and goes into panic mode.

My neurologist thinks that most of my anxiety symptoms are normal, but has decided to run an EEG because he considers it odd that I struggle to talk during an episode, or sometimes can't talk at all. The EEG is primarily precautionary, but I still want to share the adventure since the process is new to me and more than a little unusual.

Step 1: Cut your normal amount of sleep in half the night before, then abstain from caffeine the day of the test. If you know me well, you'll know sleep is essential to my well-being. I can't bring myself to comply with the four hours that will be exactly half my night's sleep, but I do cut it down to five hours (1:00 a.m. to 6:00 a.m.). Ivan stays up with me for solidarity, which is touching and useful since he wakes me up whenever I doze off.

Unfortunately, my EEG isn't until 3:30 p.m., which means that I have to do the sleep deprivation thing, skip my morning coffee, go to both therapy classes, then continue trying not to fall asleep until 3:30 in the afternoon.

Step 2: Get plugged into the machine. The technician uses some sort of salty, glue-like substance to attach numerous wires to my face, head, and neck. This wiring process takes a long time, so I have the liberty to wonder exactly how hard Ivan will have to work to get all that glue out of my hair later.

Step 3: Actually do the test. The test itself has several phases, all of which take place in a darkened room. First, I have to open and close my eyes several times. Then I have to hyperventilate for three minutes—disconcerting and rather tiring. This is followed by my favorite phase, falling asleep for twenty-five minutes. After that, the tech wakes me up for the final part of the test, which involves lots of flashing strobe lights.

We don't get the EEG results back for almost a week. When we do, they are too confusing to post on the blog. According to my neurologist, nothing is conclusive enough to rule in seizures. He also says there is nothing conclusive enough to rule them out. We decide to try seizure medication for a month to see if it will reduce the frequency or severity of my episodes. Only time will tell.

March 14th, 2017: Friction

My T-shirt and leggings are drenched. "Can't you see how hard this is for me?"

Ivan finishes rinsing the skillet.

"I'm sorry, Sayang. I thought you wanted to practice drying dishes." He reaches for the dripping plastic plate I have death-gripped in my left fist. "I can take it from here."

"This isn't about the dishes." I clutch the plate closer to my chest, then reposition it on my knee and continue scrubbing awkwardly with the dish towel. "I was talking about your job applications."

"You know I'm trying my best." Ivan adds another plate to the stack of undried dishes. "With Dr. Pickett, and the church job, and driving back and forth between twenty-seven students, you've got to cut me some slack."

"How many have you filled out today?"

"A few." He turns the faucet the wrong way and accidentally sprays suds in my face. "You realize CBU stopped paying me in March, right?" I sputter. "No offense to the School of Music, but your graduating with a B is not the end of the world. Not compared to losing our apartment." I ignore the sweat beading inside my T-shirt.

"There's always the GoFundMe . . ."

"That's not what it's for! No one asked if I was okay with that in the first place . . ."

"You were in a coma."

". . . And that's supposed to be for medical expenses, not . . . income . . ." my tongue freezes and I'm lost in the episode doctors still haven't classified.

Ivan intercepts my plate just before it joins the dish towel on the floor beside my wheelchair.

Later that day, or maybe a different day, he rocks us back and forth on the couch until my body stops shaking.

"Can't you see how hard this is for me?" I whisper, gazing at our shadows intertwined on the floor.

Part Three

June 2nd, 2017: A Job for Ivan!

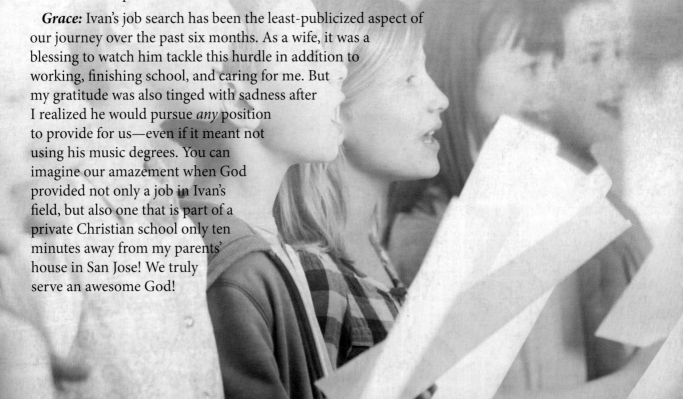

Ivan: I am extremely grateful to announce that I've accepted a position as a conservatory teacher at Valley Christian Schools! Only God could provide such a wonderful opportunity, and I'm eagerly anticipating the beginning of the school year in August.

When we realized Grace couldn't return to work, we started praying God would provide a full-time job for me since my multiple part-time jobs didn't offer medical insurance. Thus began an extensive job search in which I pursued both musical and non-musical positions.

Tomorrow marks six months since the accident, and it is mind-boggling to reflect on how far God has brought us. He truly is the God of the mountain and the valley, the ever-present help in time of trouble, and the joy of our salvation. There's so much to praise Him for. Our journey is far from over, but we thank God for the opportunity to keep focusing on His faithful provision as we move forward!

Grace: Ivan's job search has been the least-publicized aspect of our journey over the past six months. As a wife, it was a blessing to watch him tackle this hurdle in addition to working, finishing school, and caring for me. But my gratitude was also tinged with sadness after I realized he would pursue *any* position to provide for us—even if it meant not using his music degrees. You can imagine our amazement when God provided not only a job in Ivan's field, but also one that is part of a private Christian school only ten minutes away from my parents' house in San Jose! We truly serve an awesome God!

August 14th, 2017: When Your Brain Does T. Rex Arms

I risk wearing out a tired topic, but y'all deserve to know why I haven't made many public appearances since we moved to San Jose. The answer is that brains take a long time to heal, and my brain is still sensitive to overstimulation. One symptom that's made a recent comeback is T. rex arms. Speaking technically, T. rex arms is a neurological response called "posturing." Posturing is defined as "an involuntary flexion or extension of the arms [or] legs, indicating severe brain injury." One funny component of posturing is that I can't tell I'm doing it unless someone points it out. Thus, the episode below:

Last week, Mom was taking me to therapy. We stopped at Starbucks as we were running early and didn't want to sit in the waiting room forever. Mom suggested I go inside since 2:00 p.m. isn't peak coffee hour, and I'm supposed to practice short excursions to readjust to stimulation. I followed her in, feeling optimistic about my success: we were ordering to go and so it probably wouldn't take very long.

Me: taking deep breaths and focusing on a spot on the counter.

Mom: "Umm . . . can you stop doing that?"

Me, looking up at her: "What am I doing?" Then looking down: "Oh."

Behold, a perfect set of T. rex arms! After leveling a determined glare at my right arm, I forced it back down to my side. My left arm remained stubbornly glued to my chest. Our coffees happened to be ready at that precise moment, so we made a timely exit. Once outside, Mom gently pulled my left arm down.

The good news is that T. rex arms don't hurt me; they're just odd, awkward, and sometimes embarrassing. Also, unlike some other classes of patients, I'm blessed that mine only make cameo appearances under certain conditions.

We would not learn for several months that posturing arms were one sign of focal epilepsy.

September 12th, 2017: Meeting Miss Daisy

In September 2016, Ivan let me foster a feral kitten from the Riverside Humane Society. Feral kittens need extra attention and playtime since they still have undesirable wild instincts like biting and scratching. Because of this, Ivan quickly decided little Franz needed a new foster home after my accident that December. My family members were spending all their time at the hospital, and that much solitude would drive any kitten crazy. Thankfully, a friend saved the day by taking Franz (craziness included) to live with her family and their two big kitties.

As winter melted into spring, more barriers prevented Franz from coming home. Initially, it was the likelihood of infection with my compromised immune system and high dose of blood thinner. Then it was the safety hazard of kitten versus wheelchair. And finally, the transition when I was learning to walk but couldn't navigate around small things on the floor. By this time, we knew we were headed for San Jose but had no clue where we would live. Franz's foster mama saved the day again by offering to keep him *permanently*. This brought joy to my heart since I hated the idea of sending him back to the pound or giving him away to a stranger. I was positive Franz would be happy with the humans and cat friends he'd called family for the past six months.

Now fast forward to July, when one of my therapists asked if I'd consider getting a pet. She believed the therapy pet would keep me company during the solitary hours I faced with Ivan working a full-time job and my parents resuming their normal church activities. It would also provide another layer of responsibility and challenge for me as I continued resuming my wife/homemaker responsibilities. An energetic, four-legged friend would also challenge my brain to accept a higher level of stimulation as normal.

That same week I met Miss Daisy, a three-week-old, calico foster kitten. She was being raised by a family at my parents' church, and her cuteness melted my heart when she fell asleep on me after I bottle fed her. Ivan needed some reassurance that her foster family trained other therapy animals, but he eventually approved Daisy as my new pet. We waited another month till she was old enough to live in her permanent home, and Miss Daisy joined us this past Saturday. So far she is the perfect blend of cuddly naps and gentle play (I am still on blood thinner, so no biting is important!), and she presides over my home therapy with interest but not interference. Daisy and I also both sleep a lot, so you may think it's a match made in cat heaven!

November 22nd, 2017: Pie in the Sky

I don't know why we separate. Maybe I refuse help. Maybe Ivan doesn't offer. Whatever the reason, the night after Thanksgiving I abandon our scuffed blue Yaris and venture into the shadowy garage while Ivan stays in the driver's seat. We should have said goodbye to my parents' "Leftover Feast" much earlier since I've just manifested what appears to be photo-sensitive epilepsy.

I feel guilty that a string of seizures ruined the real feast yesterday. No one said anything, but I suspect they're desperate to erase the weeks spent pacing sterile hospital hallways last December. Still, Ivan could have done a better job of getting me home before dark.

"Brrr . . . It's *cold!*" My coat's too thin for me to dally while Ivan eases out of the driver's seat and retrieves the remnants of an apple pie. So, I head for the exit several rows away. *Really, he* could *move faster if he's so worried about headlights triggering a seizure*, I fume. Ivan's slowness—"methodical-ness" if you ask him—has instigated a decent amount of conflict since we got married two years ago. Perhaps too much conflict, since I'm caught off guard by a construction truck with flashing LED lights after I huff toward the door.

Something in my gut screams *"Run!"*

"Ivan!" I feel needles tingling inside my left hand—the aura that signifies the onset of a seizure. "We need to get out of here!" He's at least three yards behind me, still cradling the apple pie. I spot a door to my right and crash through it.

"That's the wrong . . ." His voice disappears.

I've never . . . been . . . Buzzing lights, blotchy cement, and wrought iron banisters coalesce. I hear a second crash somewhere. Someone's fingers are digging into my right arm.

"Grace? Grace!"

My world sparkles around a dark figure.

"Are you okay?" Ivan's almond eyes emerge and then I find myself standing in a filthy stairwell.

The air is rancid. My legs are shaking.

"Where are we?"

"You bolted straight past that truck. We're on the second floor," Ivan releases my arm. "What now?" I force a smile. "Should we go back to the elevator?"

"The truck's probably still there." Ivan frowns. "Let's try to make it downstairs and take the back way home."

My legs aren't good with stairs. "Hey, at least we still have the pie!"

Of course, he still has the pie. We'd been proud to contribute to Mom's banquet, even if our offering was "fresh baked" from Costco since I am not able to cook anymore.

"I can't believe you still have that. Great job, Sayang!" I use his nickname to lighten the mood. "Now . . . can we head to the first floor?" Needles are jabbing the inside of my left hand again, but I estimate I can manage a half-flight of stairs. *The aura could always go away,* I lie to myself.

I barely make it to the hallway. Then there's a violent thud. Air slices through my lungs.

Something's spinning behind my eyes.

"Why am I . . .?" I'm slammed against the wall. The only barrier between me and the dog-stained floor is Ivan's hyper-extended left arm. His right arm brandishes the pie like an Olympic torch.

"It was the only way to keep you from falling and hitting your head. Can you walk?" Ivan sounds like he's calculating something. I choke down more air and nod. Maybe there won't be another seizure. Maybe Ivan can keep his pie.

Suddenly I'm stumbling down the hallway, clinging to his left arm and begging God for anything to distract me from the light burrowing behind my eyes, or the left leg flopping beside me like a fish, or the realization that my left hand is tingling again. Am I making it worse by focusing on the seizures? Suddenly I see the pie levitating in a golden halo below the vibrating lights. *Look . . . at . . . the . . .*

Time collapses as seizures accumulate in the filthy hallway. I no longer know where we are, or how long we've been there, or where we're going. But I remain resolute to keep myself up: Ivan and I do *everything* together. Part of me must decide that the pie is our real enemy, not the hallway, because I rally for a final effort:

"Ivan . . . that pie . . ."

"Don't worry! I promise I'll get it home."

Finally, we arrive at A-174 and Ivan grants me the comfort of semidarkness while he sheds his shoes and coat. I slump into a chair by the kitchen table without unzipping my windbreaker.

"Yes, Dad? It's Ivan. I . . . Grace . . . we're having a bit of a rough time over here." Ivan's pinning my shoulders to the chair with one hand and balancing his iPhone with the other. "We might need to head to the ER." He doesn't notice Daisy gnawing on the pie pan in the center of the table. At any other time, I'd be incensed at Ivan's understatement or Daisy's infraction. Now I'm just grateful the pie probably won't survive the night.

Perhaps I had too many seizures or I was given too many drugs at the ER. Perhaps I've erased the rest of the holidays, including my subsequent hospitalization, with the dissociative amnesia some people experience after trauma. Whatever the reason, I conclude that we threw that pie away. Perhaps Daisy ate it, or Ivan forgot to refrigerate it, or—my personal favorite—neither of us could stomach it after our horrendous night.

None of my narratives are Ivan's. He grinned a couple of weeks ago when I asked what happened to the pie:

"We ate it, of course!"

Why the Pie?

Ivan's Thoughts

Why did I hang on to that pie when my wife couldn't even stand up? It seems ludicrous to me now. Mere seconds after we had parked our Yaris, I saw the service truck; mere milliseconds later, said truck turned on its flashing lights. I wished Grace had turned around and gotten back in the car with me; then she could have closed her eyes until the truck lights had disappeared. I could even have driven her to the entrance of the hallway that led to our apartment.

But no. Grace was the proverbial "deer in the headlights." She headed in the opposite direction of safety, namely, the stairwell. I knew that once her full-body seizures kicked in—the kind that made her entire body as limp as a dish rag—the stairwell would be the last place she should be. It would be nearly impossible for her to make her way down that stairwell, then down the long hallway that led to a breezeway, then across the breezeway, then finally down our hallway to our front door. This was turning into a small-scale disaster.

I ran after her into the stairwell, clutching the Pie of Pies. Really, there was nothing special about this half-eaten apple pie. But in the middle of that situation, my brain was in full alert mode, focusing all my attention on somehow getting Grace home. It never occurred to me to drop the pie.

I realize now that this is what Grace wished I had done. That way I could have supported her with two arms instead of one. Perhaps any other sane adult would have deduced this and dropped the pie immediately. But no. I buttressed it with one arm all the way back home. Never mind that this meant I had to keep pinning Grace to the wall every few steps the entire way home, just to keep her from falling. If anyone had seen us, that person would have thought I was mugging her.

I don't remember how many seizures Grace had during that walk. My memory says at least ten, each lasting a minute or two. Our progress was painstaking: make it a few steps, seizure, wait; repeat. Those couple hundred yards from the Yaris to our front door felt like a mile.

Somehow, we finally made it home, and I had a chance to call Grace's parents for reinforcements before taking Grace to the ER.

Looking back, I still ask myself, "Why did I hang on to the pie?"

Perhaps, in the midst of all that fear and chaos, the pie was a tangible symbol of normalcy. Perhaps it represented my ability to control the situation. It was a guarantee of imminent safety.

"How?" you may ask.

Somehow, deep in the recesses of my mind, I had convinced myself that I could save both Grace *and* the pie. After all, people only drop pies when something is wrong. If I had dropped the pie, that would have meant that Grace was beyond my help.

My one task was to save the pie—and Grace.

My Series of Unfortunate Events I

November 2017: My color-coded list of symptoms reflects menacingly under the fluorescent lights in Kaiser Redwood City's Epilepsy Clinic. The list grows almost daily, keeping eerie pace with the seizures Ivan and I read about in *The Cleveland Guide to Epilepsy*:

- Temporary loss of awareness or consciousness.
- Uncontrolled muscle movements, muscle jerking, loss of muscle tone.
- Blank stare or "staring into space" look.
- Temporary confusion, slowed thinking, problems with talking and understanding.
- Changes in hearing, vision, taste, smell, feelings of numbness or tingling.
- Problems talking or understanding.
- Lip-smacking, chewing motion, rubbing hands, finger motions.

"Oh my," says the woman with a soft German accent, a loose blond braid stroking her white coat as she shakes her head. "This looks serious. It's hard to get into the Epilepsy Monitoring Unit at short notice, but I'll see what I can do."

We leave Dr. Weber's office with an appointment for five days of continuous EEG monitoring at Kaiser Redwood City's EMU, starting Monday.

December 2017: The Transport Chair

"A transport chair is a wheelchair for short distances," my occupational therapist explains one wintery afternoon. "It's not like you'd use it all the time."

I don't remember who suggests the transport chair first, but our head-spinning night in the hallway solidifies the need. I can't risk another outing without a safety plan in case I have seizures, especially since Mom takes me out the most. I'm several inches taller than Mom.

When the chair arrives promptly from Amazon ("Only *two days!*" Mom marvels), its unwieldy cardboard box undoes my year of painstaking progress. Who cares that I'll only be using it when Mom takes me out? To everyone we meet, I'll be just another "poor thing" in a wheelchair.

"You'll be so much safer now!" my parents gush as Ivan cuts through layers of cardboard and sheaths of bubble wrap, revealing a narrow chair with tiny wheels.

Short distances, I think.

Then I realize that they are all waiting for my reaction, preferably a reaction that mirrors their own.

"I sure will!" I smile. "Who'd have thought I'd be back in a wheelchair almost exactly a year after the accident!" Everyone laughs. I try catching Ivan's eye but he doesn't see me.

The anniversary of my accident arrives a few days later. That's my first excuse for not posting the transport chair on the blog. Next, I say we've spent enough time writing about my seizures. Isn't my message that God works for good in all situations? What will everyone think if I announce I'm using a transport chair?

Right before the first anniversary of my survival, right before our first chance to celebrate a wedding anniversary outside a hospital, the chair is too big a failure.

Neither Ivan nor I admit this to each other—at least not yet. We honestly believe God works everything for good, so admitting our pain feels like letting everyone down: God, our families, even each other. Every day, I wake up with the transport chair outside our bedroom and pretend it's not there. Every day, Ivan wakes up and leaves for work and neither of us asks if we're okay.

My Series of Unfortunate Events II

April 2018: "It's wonderful to see you again, Grace," Dr. Weber beams. Sunlight floods a Bay-facing window. Her office is completely unlike the cramped, windowless room where I'd seen my most recent neurologist, Dr. Aspen.

"Same here." I smile nervously. Will she agree with Dr. Aspen's diagnosis that my symptoms suggest deep-brain focal epilepsy? Or will she side with his younger colleagues' opinion that my seizures are only a psychogenic response to my traumatic accident? Her choice determines whether or not I'll receive the medicine we know I need.

"I confess I don't like to work off another physician's gut diagnosis," she sighs as she glances between me and the computer, "but Dr. Aspen was seeing improvement in your symptoms after he prescribed Lamictal. Since I'm inheriting you after his retirement, I'll keep you on your epilepsy medicine and run another EEG in five years. Maybe the EEG will show some electricity then."

She smiles so warmly that I don't ask to raise my Lamictal dose, even though I'm still having multiple seizures a week. It's enough that she hasn't labeled me a psychogenic case.

"Wow, you must be her favorite patient," Ivan says as we merge onto the freeway on our way home. "I doubt she hugs all her patients at the end of their appointment."

May 20th, 2018: Seeing My Superstar

I'd been obsessed with Itzhak Perlman ever since my violin teacher lent me a recording of him when I was nine.

My obsession sparked a quest to be just like Mr. Perlman. First, I needed to practice enough to go to Juilliard and take lessons from the man himself. Second, I should go to a concert and *hear him play in person*. Mr. Perlman scheduled a concert in our small Wisconsin city when I was about thirteen. His concerts sell out everywhere, but my violin teacher got me and Mom tickets since my teacher was playing in the orchestra. I was beside myself with excitement—until the concert was canceled.

Fast-forward to my time studying violin at Eastman. When I was seventeen, I met an Eastman professor named Charles Castleman whom I admired so much that I *had* to learn from him. But even if I didn't go to Juilliard, I knew I'd find a way to Mr. Perlman. He visited Eastman in my freshman year; my dream was finally coming true! Not so. Tickets started at $90. The box office workers barely concealed their contempt for my questions: *Was there a student discount?* No. *What about rush tickets?* No. *Could I hang around in case someone no-showed?* The lady's glare told me it was time to go. Insult was added to injury since Mr. Perlman was performing in Kodak Theater, the hall where the school orchestras rehearsed every day. Now he was on that very stage, shining under those same golden lights, while I shivered outside in the cold marble hall.

Seven years later, Ivan and I live in San Jose. Can you guess who just performed with the San Francisco Symphony? Can you guess who just went? This was the biggest gamble we've made since my accident, but I just had to go. I'd known about Mr. Perlman's concert since the previous fall, and we'd been saving and planning ever since. You'd think the epilepsy diagnosis would have dissuaded me, but it did not. It didn't matter how much medication I needed. I was going to make that May performance. I didn't even care if I had seizures right as Ivan rolled my travel chair into the concert hall. Perlman or bust!

So, what happened? I did have a regrettably large number of seizures in the lobby, and Ivan did want to take me home. I didn't care. An usher helped him wheel me into my handicap spot just as the lights went down. And then Mr. Perlman made his entrance—in

a wheelchair. I knew he had health problems, but I wasn't sure how often he performed in a wheelchair. His vulnerable entrance sent shivers down my spine given how hard I'd struggled to get in the hall. Then Mr. Perlman lifted his violin and began to play. The warm tones of his Stradivarius filled every corner of the hall with Bach's exquisite phrases. His concerto was the perfection I'd always imagined.

And then my heart skipped a beat. Mr. Perlman was conducting the second piece himself. I'd assumed he would stay in his chair. I was wrong. He turned to the regular conducting podium even though it was four feet high. With large steps to reach the music stand on top, Mr. Perlman dragged himself upright so unsteadily I wondered if he'd fall. Orchestra members flinched, and I think everyone in the audience wanted someone, anyone to lend him a hand.

Except for Mr. Perlman. He grabbed a pair of crutches before twisting, wobbling, and hopping his way upward. There was a final, dangerous sway as he sat down on a chair atop the podium. After a cursory bow acknowledging the thunderous applause for his climb, he raised his hands and began milking a marvelous orchestral performance. I only had enough energy to stay a few minutes after his climb, but I'd seen enough. My superstar is super in more ways than one.

My Series of Unfortunate Events III

July 2018: "It's good to consider the facts, Grace." Dr. Weber's tone is not unkind. I study my chipped black toenail polish. Ivan and I are back in the old, cramped space where we worked with Dr. Austin last winter. Now it's summer and I'm sweating, not because it's hot but because my seizures still don't read on the EEG. One more strike against epilepsy, one more in favor of psychogenic seizures.

Last week, I'd gotten food poisoning from a bad Costco salad and gone into *status epilepticus*—a potentially fatal state of continuous seizures. That's what they told me in the ER. After they held me overnight to run a twenty-four-hour EEG, they said they couldn't find any abnormalities.

"There's just no electricity." Dr. Weber sighs.

"What about Dr. Aspen's theory that Grace has deep-brain focal epilepsy?" Ivan interjects.

"Honestly, I would've expected to see *something* after an episode like this." Dr. Weber frowns. "But you say your medication is still helping?"

"Sort of." I shrug. "I can't go out much because I'm so sensitive to flashing lights and LED headlights." I pray she'll raise my dose of Lamictal, the drug that's proven to help my light sensitivity.

"And your psychologist says you don't meet the criteria for psychogenic seizures?"

"You didn't get his letter?"

"No, I got it." She smiles half-heartedly. "Hang in there, Grace. I wish there was more I could do."

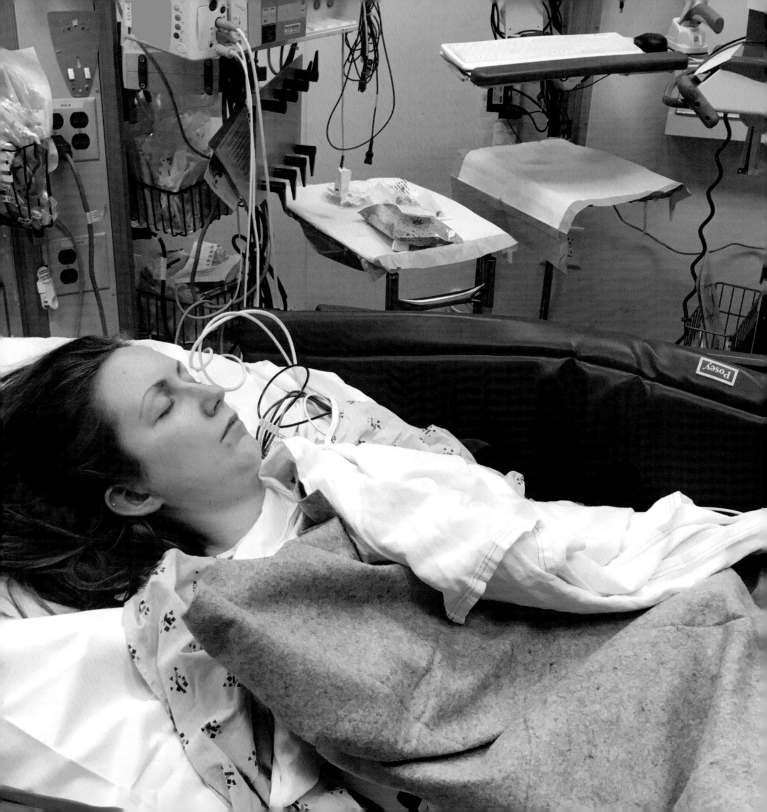

January 2019: Not Stanford

Am I dying? Oxygen hovers out of reach. My throat constricts. My nostrils transfix.

When I wake up in the emergency room breathing through an oxygen tube, I know I'm not going home. It's my second ER trip in three days. The next seizure starts seconds after I can't name the date—a basic measure of cognitive awareness. I've already had a lot of seizures earlier in the night, according to Ivan. At least six.

Two years of seizures has won me notoriety among Northern Californian neurologists for my severe light sensitivity. Tonight is different. Tonight, my seizures have no trigger—and they're big. When my medication works, flashing lights trigger little seizures in my left hand (neurologists calls them "focal"), but I transitioned to generalized seizures three days ago. I'd drop like a rag doll and fade in and out of consciousness, gasping for breath. Tonight, I'm having seizures back-to-back and I stop breathing altogether. The 911 operator coaches Ivan through CPR to keep me breathing until the ambulance arrives.

There are some perks to being an *emergency* emergency, though. I'm too disoriented (neurologists call it "post-ictal") to care at the time, but I've scored a large, critical care room instead of the cramped ER cubicle I landed two days ago. Ivan and my family even secure blue, vinyl-backed chairs for the vigil everyone suspects will stretch into the night.

A nurse times my next seizure on his watch before beginning a barrage of questions. "Does she usually have seizures like this?" His accent is recognizable, probably Indian, and he's speaking softly to keep everyone calm. "No."

Why the heck would we be here if this was normal?

"What does she normally do?"

"Her left hand normally clenches tightly, then she freezes and can't talk."

I'd usually confirm that the nurse is updating my chart, but my eyes are screwed shut against the merciless fluorescent lights.

"So, no falling, no lack of consciousness, no inability to breathe?"

"No, not at all."

I wish Ivan had asked about my chart. If my brain weren't so exhausted from following the conversation, my romantic side might also resent how coolly and professionally Ivan is handling this near-death situation. But, for the moment, all I hope for is that he's given all the necessary information, and that my medical record works for me, not against me.

Doctors had called my physical and mental recovery miraculous—until the seizures started last year. The seizures themselves weren't surprising since epilepsy is common in stroke and brain-injury patients, and I've suffered both. But my EEG didn't show abnormal electricity, the gold standard for diagnosing epilepsy. The younger epileptologists at my neurology clinic in Redwood City concluded that the seizures must be induced by psychological trauma—even though my symptoms looked epileptic and I screened out of PTSD in several psychiatric evaluations.

One epileptologist—the one who bothered talking *to* me as an individual instead of *at* me as a patient—didn't accept their diagnosis. Dr. Aspen argued that some epilepsy is so deep in the brain it doesn't show up on EEGs. His snowy hair suggested he'd been researching the disease long before EEGs became the last word on epilepsy or my other doctors finished med school . But even his decades of expertise couldn't clear me. He retired before he found the right mix of medication for my seizures, and I was assigned to a younger epileptologist who was nonplussed by Dr. Aspen's hypothesis. She rewrote my chart so that "epilepsy" was at the bottom and "Conversion Disorder with Attacks or Seizures" was at the top. To anyone who hadn't talked to Dr. Aspen, I was a psych patient who panicked around lights, then lost control of my body. The fact that epilepsy drugs provided measurable relief was merely an inconvenient detail.

"ATTENTION—STROKE ALERT. ATTENTION—STROKE ALERT." The intercom jerks me back to consciousness after my next seizure. If the ER doctor skims the top of my chart while rushing between crises, he won't take my case seriously. But if the nurse documented Ivan's answers well, the doctor might read to the bottom and order the epileptic rescue drug we know will stop the seizures.

I squeeze my eyes shut. Maybe I can block out the searing lights a bit. Maybe I can even fall asleep and circumvent the next seizure. No such luck. My body goes limp, my lungs seize, the room fades. . . . Then my body belongs to me again and my dad's voice is pounding me back to my senses:

"And just why haven't you given her a rescue drug yet? She got it the last time she was here. You can't let her keep having seizures."

"Well, there's a narcotics shortage under the current administration." This man's sterile tone suggests that he's the supervising doctor.

"Whatever. I know you have the drug. Don't you think twelve seizures is enough?" Even my post-ictal brain admires Dad's strategy. At 6' 4," with two decades in upper-level management, he usually gets what he wants. Both he and the doctor know the hospital can't risk a patient complaint in a case of my magnitude, even if this facility specializes in orthopedics instead of neurology. Hospitals in our area serve the upscale residents of the Silicon Valley, residents who'd be outraged to imagine the local ER botching their own treatment. The fact that the ambulance rushed me to this facility since it's only five minutes from our apartment makes no difference. This hospital—and this doctor—is officially liable for my case.

But there's one rebuttal to Dad's argument. If I'm hiding the fact that I have a mental disorder—if these seizures are psychogenic—why should the hospital waste that precious drug on me? Has the doctor seen Dr. Aspen's notes and his epilepsy diagnosis? Or has he only skimmed the top of my chart? "Conversion Disorder" would justify ignoring me no matter how many more times my lungs constrict. Only epilepsy patients get rescue drugs.

"Well, I can't give her anything until we do a CT scan to rule out other neurological events," the doctor hedges.

"And how long will that take?" Dad's tone hasn't lost its bite. Processing CT scans can take several hours.

"Radiology's pretty slow tonight so I'll send her right down."

"You do that. But, in the meantime, I'd appreciate you locating that drug and calling around for a different facility to take Grace. We both know you're not equipped to treat her."

This last barb tips the scales in my favor. Regardless of how thoroughly the man has read my chart, he clearly dreads a patient complaint about *his* incompetence—a complaint we have every right to make if I spend the night in an orthopedics hospital.

The CT scan probably goes smoothly, but I've had too many seizures to notice. My mind only has space for two thoughts: *When will I get the rescue drug?* and *Where will they send me?*

When I get back to my room there is no rescue drug, although someone's finally dimmed the lights. I have a clean CT, of course. None of us believed the doctor's suggestion that I might have had a stroke during all those seizures. I doubt anyone in the ER believed him.

Perhaps he was following the protocol for patients who faint, but it seems more likely he was looking for another excuse to delay giving me the rescue drug. No neurologist has ever confused my seizures with strokes or fainting.

Ceding the rescue drug as a lost cause, my family corners the doctor for a second round of negotiations. This time Ivan takes the lead. He's a master of suggestion, and few doctors can withstand Ivan and Dad as a team.

"Excuse me?" Ivan clears his throat.

"Yes." The doctor's abrupt tone implies he's steeled for a second conflict. "I just wanted to check and see where you're sending my wife?"

"Oh, we haven't gotten around to that yet."

"I completely understand you're busy. But her CT is back, and there's no reason for her to take up a bed when you're so full. Do you mind transferring her to the Kaiser at Redwood City? That's where she's usually seen."

Smart idea! It's been at least twenty minutes since my last seizure, so my head is clear enough to realize these new seizures are probably large enough to read on an EEG machine. An inpatient stay at my regular clinic would be the quickest route to proving I have epilepsy, not psychogenic seizures.

"We'll call around, but I can't guarantee anything. I have to send her wherever they have open beds. Redwood City is our primary site, but we also have contracts with Stanford and UC San Francisco . . ." Their voices vanish as Ivan follows him down the hall.

Stanford was the first hospital to label me a psychiatric case, even before Redwood City. A San Jose ER doctor transferred me there eighteen months ago, on a night much like this one. That night, I was convulsing repeatedly, and Stanford had the only open bed with an EEG unit. Stanford epileptologists were the first to ignore my clean psychiatric evaluation and decide that my "normal" EEG indicated the seizures were psychogenic. All I had to do was admit that I had a mental health disorder, and trust that the seizures would go away on their own. Those doctors didn't care that I'd spent a meager eighteen hours in their unit. EEG evaluations often last days before specialists reach a conclusion. I quickly learned how unlikely Kaiser's epileptologists were to question an elite hospital like Stanford—all except Dr. Aspen.

But Dr. Aspen retired over a year ago, and now I might be headed back to the doctors who'd first dismissed me as a girl in denial. Part of me claims that these new seizures are God's answer to our prayers: they will show up on the EEG and prove that I haven't endured two years of self-inflicted suffering by denying the truth. But a different part of me whispers that if I'm sent to Stanford, it won't matter what kind of seizures I'm having. I'll always be the girl who lies about her mental health.

Suddenly, Ivan's face is bending over mine. "Hey, it looks as though you haven't had a seizure in a while! Maybe you're slowing down on your own. They're looking for a place to send you." He must be forcing himself to sound energetic: It's almost 1:30 a.m.

"Where is everyone?"

"Mom and Dad went home. They'll meet us in the morning. I'll text them once the hospital places you."

"You're not leaving, right?"

"Of course not! I've got a substitute teacher for tomorrow morning." He brushes some tears off my cheek with his thumb. "The nurse is calling around right now to see what beds are open. And who knows? They might even have a bed in UC San Francisco. Their researchers haven't seen you yet. Redwood City could also be good." He ignores the obvious third option.

"Ivan?" I try not to let my voice wobble. "Don't let them send me to Stanford." He looks away.

The lights above my bed flare up and a new nurse pops her head in. The shifts must have changed.

"Great news!" She's clearly high on coffee. "It was super hard to get you in anywhere, but we managed to pull some strings. Stanford only has one bed open, and you're the lucky one who's going to get it!"

I groan and turn my face to the wall. "Do you mind dimming the lights?" Her startled look reminds me that I'm supposed to act relieved. "And that's nice about Stanford."

"Transport will be here soon!" She flits away, apparently satisfied with my gratitude. The lights are still blazing.

"Ivan?" He's facing the other way, reading a flyer about heart disease he must have pulled off the wall somewhere. "Can you turn the lights off—all the way?"

I won't let him see that I am crying.

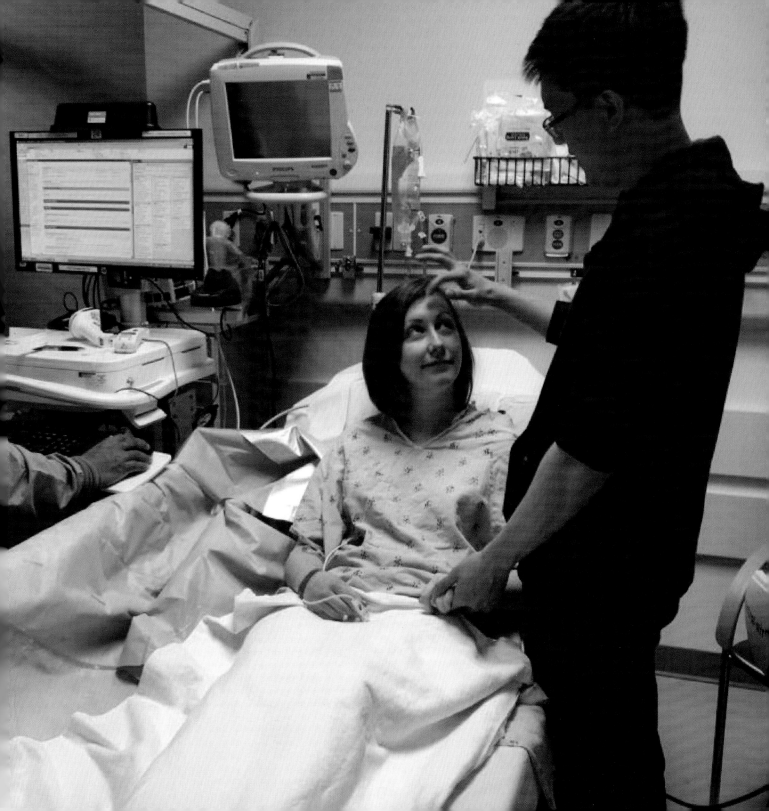

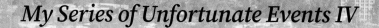

My Series of Unfortunate Events IV

February 2019: The doctor who treated me after I arrived at Stanford said they had a new research program for patients like me. I pray Dr. Weber will write the rare, out-of-network referral. It sounds perfect: I get the twenty-four weeks of cognitive behavioral therapy they've suggested, and we'll get the epilepsy research we've requested.

"That sounds very interesting, Grace." Dr. Weber's face broadens into a warm smile.

"We're wondering if you can match us to a specific doctor, given the unique nature of Grace's case," Ivan ventures. "Have you heard of a Dr. Arianna Key?"

"Oh! Arianna Key." Dr. Weber's eyes crinkle in recognition. "We used to work together when I was at Stanford. Very capable woman."

Ivan nods. "She seems to be one of the top scientists researching the boundary between epileptic and nonepileptic seizures."

"Unfortunately, I can't guarantee who you'll see once you get to Stanford." She laughs softly. "But I can write a referral. In fact, I'll write it today!"

I receive a written referral to Stanford two months later.

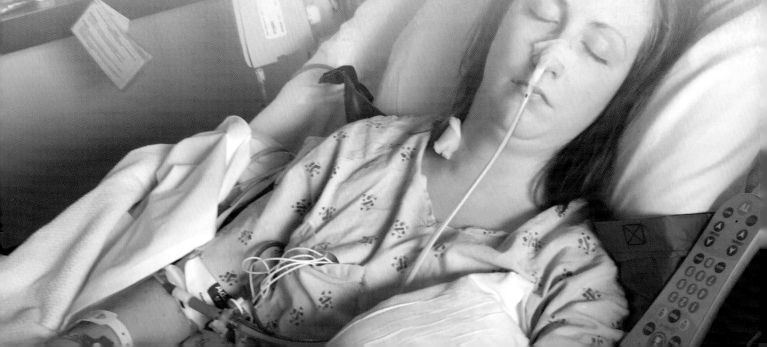

There is nothing worse than watching a loved one suffer. When I married Grace, I pledged to do my utmost to keep her safe and happy. In the face of seizures, ER trips, and flawed diagnoses, I was failing. Grace was not safe, and "happiness" was just a word in the dictionary. I desperately wished I could take Grace's pain away from her, that I could restore all her physical abilities. I wished I could banish her neurological deficits to the four corners of the earth and give her back the precious music she had lost. I wished we faced a bright future of new adventures, not a bleak one of endless struggle.

Even as Grace and I bounced from hospital to hospital and doctor to doctor, we knew our lives were held securely in the palm of God's hand. I don't mean we were in a constant state of meditation on God's sovereignty and peace; it was often easy to be distracted or distressed by the specifics of a particular situation. (Did that ER doctor *really* write an accurate report of Grace's symptoms? What if her neurologist thinks we just freaked out prematurely?) The only reason Grace kept going, the only reason I kept going, was that God Himself was strengthening our hearts to endure this struggle, whether or not we were always conscious of it.

While waiting on our referral to Stanford, I prayed Grace would receive an accurate diagnosis leading to accurate treatment. I prayed that the Stanford doctors would respect Grace and do their best to understand her symptoms *and* her point of view. Perhaps God might use their expertise to bring an end to Grace's suffering. More than anything, I prayed that God would give me and Grace the strength to worship Him, follow Him, and trust Him no matter what.

April-August 2019: *The Idles of Summer*

Name: *Grace Utomo.* **Date:** *April 6th, 2019.* I hope Dr. Key[4] doesn't think my handwriting is erratic. Ivan's implored me to whip through her seven-page intake questionnaire so I can close my eyes afterward. The light flickering in the lobby ceiling might trigger a seizure. He was even more adamant about me closing my eyes during the headlight-riddled drive to Palo Alto. I don't blame him: We've waited months for this appointment. Dr. Key's bio on Stanford Medical Center's website touts her "state of the art" research on formerly undiagnosable seizure disorders and lists a plethora of awards, including "Humanism and Excellence in Teaching."

"Give me a few minutes, please." Dr. Key begins scrutinizing my questionnaire as soon as she unlocks her office. She wears almost no makeup and twists her sandy hair into a black clip that slides further down her neck each time she turns her head. The office is similarly colorless except for a generic pink lamp. I don't see any photos of family, not even pets. Nothing to distract from her plethora of diplomas papering the wall beside the exit; nothing except for a forgettable quote from Jung.

As she flips to the second page, I crane my neck to see if I can make out the building's entrance or the parking lot below. But all Dr. Key's blinds are shut. I have no way of knowing which clinic houses one of Stanford's most elite neuroscientists.

"So, let me get this right." Dr. Key must have skipped to the end of the questionnaire while I was spying. "You say you're not able to perform any independent activities due to light-triggered seizures." She frowns. "Like, *any?* Even short errands?"

I nod.

"And the medical records from your last neurologist say EEG brain scans show no electricity. She recommends psychotherapy. But then we have a note from your psychologist saying you don't qualify for therapy since you don't have depression, anxiety, or PTSD."

I nod again.

Dr. Key unlocks a creaky steel cabinet and tosses my questionnaire inside. "Lucky for you, I'd agree with your psychologist. This questionnaire is almost 100 percent accurate at identifying psychiatric instability." She smiles. "Basically, you're my ideal patient. No traditional epilepsy, no overt mood disorder. I'd *love* to study—*treat*—you. Are we good to start next week?" I smile. Her enthusiasm almost camouflages the fact that she's a doctor.

"There's only one condition." She scribbles on a notepad. "I need you to do something independent before next week. It's just some data for the study I'm doing." Dr. Key smiles reassuringly. "Don't worry too much. I can't wait to start digging into your case."

❖

"Hey Mom?" My eyes are closed but I can tell she's freshening her lipstick. Mom's Southern manners are intractable even though she knows these last-minute touches are unnecessary: Dr. Key doesn't allow family in appointments.

"Can we park away from the flashing construction lights so I can walk around the parking lot by myself?"

"Are you sure that's a good idea?" She smacks her lips. "You just opened your eyes on the freeway for the first time last week."

"Dr. Key wants me to keep pushing myself to be independent. It's part of her study." Mom cranks the car and we roll down several spaces before she parks a second time. "Her other patients have seizures when they get nervous." I open my eyes. "I have to keep making myself nervous for her to keep believing my seizures are only triggered by light."

I notice a sign posted a few rows down and decide to make a lap, then head inside. The laminated sign is a goal more than anything else, but that changes when I read it. NOTICE: PAYMENT REQUIRED TO PARK IN THIS ROW. "Mom?" I forget our independence exercise and rush back to her. "Are you *paying* to park here?"

"Oh no! That's the wonderful thing about your seizures. Disability permits are exempt. Everyone else pays."

Then I turn to face the clinic with my eyes open for the first time. Swank, mid-2000s architecture, just like Mom said. The sign above the entrance proclaims PSYCHIATRY & BEHAVIORAL SCIENCES in wrought iron.

❖

"We didn't want to worry you!" Mom and Ivan remonstrate when I interrogate them separately about the psychiatry building in the afternoon and evening. Mom follows with an optimistic "Dr. Key sounds sincere!" Ivan simply shrugs. "She's the best in her field," he says, "no matter where she works."

Dr. Key's assignments vary but their import is the same: trigger as many seizures as necessary to desensitize me to the trigger. If I *feel* less nervous around lights, my seizures should go away. "I thought we might have already narrowed down the problem to neurological light sensitivity instead of, you know, anxiety . . ." I stammer after my third round of stress tests. Dr. Key reorganizes some papers on her oversize oak desk and notes that "sensitivity" is a very subjective term. I engineer a smile which I hope conceals my frustration. We'd attributed her first few stress tests to due diligence before moving on to treating my light sensitivity. But now Ivan and I wonder if Dr. Key *needs* some of my seizures to be triggered by anxiety. When her methods don't change although my seizures continue to be triggered only by light, we do some research of our own. A little web surfing uncovers a recent lecture she'd given on *subconscious* mood disorders. I should have known. I'd read the wrought iron sign.

"*Ivan*, it's the parking lot." It's July, and my husband has taken over my biweekly Stanford appointments since school is out. "Just a couple of laps and we'll go in," I bargain. Ivan stays glued to the driver's seat. "Sure, my sessions aren't going great, but these walks are one nice thing to do while we're out here."

Silence.

"Just admit it, this landscaping is way better than wandering around downtown San Jose. Now, can't we take a nice walk under those trees?" I point to a walkway shaded by sycamores and eucalyptus. The air sags with perfume, although something about the blend is too saturated this week. Ivan sighs and trails me half-heartedly along the path, flinching every time an anxious driver whips by searching for a spot.

As summer fades and my seizures remain, very few assignments merit their risk in Ivan's eyes. "Why keep staring into LED lights when you know that won't desensitize you?" he asks as we wander the parking lot before my second-to-last appointment. The mid-August asphalt bakes our skin. "You know she's more interested in doing whatever with your subconscious than in treating your actual seizures." I squeeze his hand. A summer of tangled hypotheses is the opposite of what we envisioned that first Monday when Ivan guided me inside with my eyes closed. But Dr. Key is the best in her field. Do we have another choice?

An Additional Comment from Grace

Choice is a fairy tale, a game that helps us fall asleep at night, like discovering we're sole heirs of an unknown great uncle and have just inherited his Hawaiian mansion. Choice is for couples with budding careers and sleek, upgraded cars, maybe a kid on the way. Ivan and I, however, never seem to choose where we go or what we do: my future unfolds one inscrutable day at a time, with past disappointments closing in relentlessly behind us. All we can do is sprint, hoping our dash is mad enough to keep up.

This helplessness feeds new anger and bitterness in my heart, emotions I thought God had protected me from during my initial recovery.

"Why, God?" I cry out each day as my Stanford treatment approaches an unsatisfactory close. I might be journaling in my bedroom, or practicing physical therapy exercises on the living room floor. Today, I'm eating a peanut butter sandwich with no one but Miss Daisy for company. "Why did you save my life if I'm going to be misunderstood and stuck inside forever? Why didn't you just give me regular epilepsy?"

Occasionally, I hear updates from my parents about fellow church members who've had accidents or been diagnosed with diseases. I'd never admit it, but I envy these poor souls: at least everyone agrees on what's wrong with them. No one blames them for their suffering.

God could cure me of my bitterness and envy on the spot. He doesn't. The following year, I'll read Psalm 119:11: "I have stored up your word in my heart, that I might not sin against you." Ivan and I memorized the whole of the Letter to the Philippians while we were dating, but I'd assumed I had lost the ability to memorize anything after the brain injury. Spurred on by Psalm 119, I'll decide to try again, even if I only get through a verse or two a month. Psalm 139 captures my attention because it describes how God is the only One who can rescue me from bitterness and depression:

If I say, "Surely the darkness shall cover me,
and the light about me be night,"
even the darkness is not dark to you;
the night is bright as the day,
for darkness is as light with you.
(Ps. 139:11-12)

Copying these words—and eventually the entire Psalm—every day for over a year forces me to meditate on the Word of God no matter how I'm feeling. God will use this discipline to show me I *do* have a choice about how my life goes. I may not have as many choices as most college-educated, first-world, twenty-somethings. But I have the most important choice: will I give up and obey my sinful emotions when things aren't going my way? Or will I ask for God to deliver me from both trials and temptations, trusting that the darkness in my soul is nothing compared to the light of His mercy and grace? Psalm 139 doesn't promise a happily-ever-after ending for every trial. But it does reassure us that understanding God's character and how He demonstrates love for each of His children is more than enough to sustain us in every trial and temptation.

June-August 2019: Light and Darkness

Our apartment darkens gradually. At first its fluorescent lights blaze overhead for days at a time or for however long I stay inside avoiding the flashing LEDs that trigger seizures when I go out.

Our lights only stay on a day or two at a time once one of my migraines lasts ten days in a row. Sometimes, they last even longer. My brain is so complex that Imitrex, the gold standard for aborting migraines, often fails.

When one migraine expands to twenty-one days, I learn the meaning of "Let nature take its course." The injection at Urgent Care only lasts four hours. The IV cocktail at the ER doesn't work. The steroid prescription helps a little—but only six days later.

"All headaches stop eventually," Dr. Weber observes.

After two months of a continuous migraine, I decide our fluorescent overheads are mocking me. The only light I can tolerate is from three incandescent IKEA lamps. We can't find one for the bathroom; so, I shower in the dark.

"Please . . . you're a neuroscientist just like Dr. Key. Isn't there anything else you can give me?" I beg Dr. Weber over the phone.

"I'm sorry, Grace." Her voice is flat. "There's only so much Western medicine can do."

Western medicine.

I've heard of people practicing mindfulness for pain management. After my accident, doctors even suggested it might help my TBI anxiety. I didn't follow through on it since my anxiety decreased with time, but now those chronic pain testimonials sound appealing.

Mindfulness can't hurt any worse than my migraine.

I do a little research and download the Headspace app on my iPhone. At first, the practice seems monotonous, even bizarre. Can closing my eyes and counting breaths for ten or fifteen minutes really lessen the pain? Unlike all those medications, mindfulness works. My brain can't count my breaths and register the migraine simultaneously, so I find myself enjoying a few pain-free minutes each morning.

Three months into the migraine, I remember the fountain. Mom and I used to pass the oblong, granite-and-cobblestone fixture every day on our way to the complex's gym. Its trickle played a calming counterpoint to the sizzling summer heat. What if the fountain soothes my head the same way mindfulness does? I certainly need some sort of link to the outside world: I've only burrowed deeper into my dark apartment after we observed that light-triggered seizures perpetuate the migraine.

The air is already simmering when Mom leads me to the fountain one bright August morning. My head is pounding its usual death march. But the water smells fresh, even before I open my eyes. It sounds as pure as crystal. Ripples hypnotize my watering eyes when I blink them open. *Feel your lungs expand on the "in" breath, and your body release on the "out" breath,* the mindfulness track echoes in my mind.

"Grace? Grace? Are you okay?" My vacant expression must have mimicked how I look before a seizure.

"Yes, Mom." The throbbing in my head evaporates like a malevolent mist. "I'm perfect."

Ivan's Thoughts

I respect doctors. Treating something as complex as the human brain fascinates me like nothing else. There is no other organ like it; physiologically, it is the closest link we have to our inner, immaterial selves. In my junior year of high school, I was so interested in the human brain that I actually thought about majoring in neuroscience instead of music. Providentially, music won out.

I still respect doctors a lot. Although God is our perfect Healer, doctors bear the earthly burden of restoring their fellow creatures to good health. Sometimes they succeed, but not always. Their work is serious and unpredictable, so doctors deserve our respect and gratitude.

Grace and I never asked for this "privilege," but we've worked with many doctors from a wide range of disciplines. God has graciously provided access to tertiary-level medical care every time Grace has needed it. Years of interaction with this type of medical provider have also taught us a "civilian" metric that's extremely important. We've discovered that doctors generally fall into two camps with regard to interpersonal interactions, or "bedside manners."

I have seen highly intelligent doctors treat Grace as if she were a complex collection of statistics. I have seen other highly intelligent doctors show compassion in their eyes, in their voices, in the extra time they took to field our myriad questions. We've been assigned to doctors who work so fast they could bill by the minute—and if Grace happens to improve, what a happy coincidence. On the other hand, God has also blessed us with doctors who spend extra time conversing with us as intellectual equals, rather than reciting facts.

As Grace's time working with Dr. Key draws to an end, all of us—Grace, her mother, and I—finally admit we're driving straight for a brick wall with a giant, faded question mark painted right in the center of it:

Now what?

We'd hoped—perhaps assumed—that God intended to use Grace's time at Stanford to set her diagnosis straight, find the right treatment for her seizures, maybe even address other harmful symptoms like migraines. That hope is rapidly diminishing. We can no longer ignore that Dr. Key is treating Grace for a psychiatric disorder instead of her light-triggered seizures. Is God reminding us yet again that He is the only One who holds the answers? After all, doctors are only human.

August 8th, 2019: A Pleasant Patient

The truth will set you free. I exhale slowly. God wouldn't lie, right? *This is our last chance, Lord,* I plead as I rearrange my hair in the bathroom mirror. I take another deep breath, copy one of those "power stances" they recommend on YouTube. "Okay. It's showtime."

Dr. Key meets me outside the bathroom.

"Oh hi," I try sounding nonchalant, "it's great to see you." Silence.

"Do you want to chat by ourselves first?" I ask. "Or should Ivan join right away?"

"Whatever makes you comfortable." Her smile is as pale as her pink cardigan.

Whatever makes you *comfortable,* I retort mentally. Outwardly, I smile. Ivan and I agree our last chance at any concession that my seizures are light-triggered lies in letting Dr. Key run the appointment.

"Can I talk with you first, then pull Ivan in later?" This is the answer she's looking for, although I would rather have Ivan with me the whole time. Recently, Dr. Key's completely overlooked all the test results that confirm light is my only seizure trigger.

"Of course." Her voice softens, almost imperceptibly.

Lord, please help me, I pray as we round the corner to her office. My latest migraine is pounding furiously, hammering into oblivion all the arguments that seemed straightforward when Ivan reviewed them with me in the car.

Dr. Key's office glows an uncanny shade of red when she unlocks her door. She gestures to the afternoon light reaching a few persistent fingers through the blinds.

"Sorry. I have windows closed for privacy. The construction's on our side today."

"That's okay. I have a really awful migraine."

"I can see it in your eyes."

My migraine doesn't win a respite from her characteristic drilling: *How many seizures this week?* Four. *How many light triggers?* Five. *How many anxiety triggers?* Zero. *How did I feel before and after I saw the bright lights?* Her tone sharpens when I reply "Normal."

"Well, it looks like you fit the profile for Functional Neurological Disorder," Dr. Key pronounces after a weighty pause.

I open my mouth to argue but my throbbing head protests. "Can we bring Ivan in?"

"Of course." Dr. Key's smile fades and she rises abruptly. The door slams on her exit.

Lord, please *let the truth set us free,* I pray. Then . . .

"So, I was just explaining to your wife that she's the classic FND profile." Dr. Key continues as she readjusts her ergonomically correct chair and Ivan slides into the faux-tweed seat next to mine. "Do you have any questions?"

Ivan clears his throat. "As a matter of fact, I do."

"That's wonderful." Dr. Key's smile seems genuine this time. "How can I help?"

"Well, you say Grace matches the classic FND profile. But from the research presentation you sent at the beginning of the summer, her light-triggered seizures seem like the opposite of FND mood-triggered ones. Plus, hers started improving when you prescribed a new epilepsy drug, while the presentation said epilepsy drugs don't help FND seizures." I admire that Ivan substitutes "you sent" for "you delivered." Much less accusatory. "Can you help me understand how she fits the FND profile?"

Now Dr. Key clears her throat.

"I see you missed your calling as a neuroscientist." No one laughs. "Well, FND is such a fringe disorder that it's hard to categorize. There's so much we still don't know about the brain."

"That's just it. We've always heard Grace's seizures aren't hard to categorize, at least visually. We've always been told they look like textbook epilepsy." Ivan tugs at the collar of his striped polo. "The sticking point is they don't read on the EEG. What if *that's* the part we don't understand about the brain?"

I recross my ankles and my head pounds harder. This is the point where Dr. Key would lose her temper with me if we were alone. The clock on the wall ticks unbearably loudly.

"I can see how you would think that."

"Really?" Ivan almost relaxes.

"Language is subjective. When I say Grace is 'classic FND' and others say her seizures look 'textbook epileptic,' you probably hear what you want to hear. I don't know what context people have said that in, so I can't comment. All I know is that her seizures are psychiatric based on the three months of research I have done."

That's NOT what you said all summer! I want to shout. *What about being the light-sensitive case you said you'd never seen before?* Ivan's eyebrows remind me that interrupting is not part of the plan.

"I thought the research says you can't diagnose someone with FND simply because their seizures don't read on an EEG machine. I thought there has to be positive evidence of a psychiatric disorder as well." Ivan answers Dr. Key without missing a beat.

"Grace is just one of those really clear-cut cases." She turns to me abruptly. "Here's your copy of the letter I sent to Kaiser."

I scan the glossy paper in my hand, foolishly hoping it might say something other than what Dr. Key just had.

"I just . . . I don't know if I need a psychologist since you said I don't have a mood disorder," I counter, finally remembering which argument Ivan had assigned me. "We understand you've put your professional expertise into this summer " (here I falter). Ivan pats my hand. ". . . but since my seizures remain light-triggered and psychotherapy remains, um, ineffective, would you consider removing the recommendation for future psychiatric supervision?"

"I thought you might say that." Now both Ivan and I stiffen. "Did you finish reading the letter? It says psychiatric supervision *as needed*. I'm sure you can work something out with your neurologist so you don't see a psychologist if you don't want to." Dr. Key leans back in her chair triumphantly.

So, I don't see one unless my neurologist *wants me to,* I correct mentally. We all know Dr. Weber has the highest opinion of Dr. Key's research.

"Well, that's about all the time we have for today. Take care, Grace." She half nods to Ivan. "I wish you the best of luck." Her voice has no ice in it as she locks the door behind us. I stand in the hall, immobile, gaping at the letter. Why does she begin by calling me a "pleasant patient"? Being nice didn't matter in the long run. The truth didn't set me free.

I grab Ivan's hand and tow him toward the exit.

My Series of Unfortunate Events V

August 2019

Grace,

I am an Epilepsy specialist and seeing surgical Epilepsy patients.

So, I would like to ask you to find a neurologist in San Jose who can guide you with treatment of migraine headache.

You can keep me in the loop, and I am more than happy to help, but I should not be your primary neurologist.

Sincerely,

Erika S. Weber MD.

❖

Hi Dr. Weber,

This is Ivan writing for Grace. I hope you're well. Grace's brain injury makes it hard for her to express herself assertively so I want to help her.

She's been having a migraine for three and a half weeks, perpetuated with every new seizure (around two per week). We understand that you're an epilepsy specialist and that Grace's events are non-epileptic. However, if I remember correctly, you also work in the neurology clinic. We would prefer to stay in your care since, every time we connect with a new doctor, we have to go over so much medical history that it hinders Grace from getting the help she needs. Furthermore, San Jose referred Grace to Redwood City because they felt unqualified to treat her non-epileptic seizures. However, if you still think it best to pass us off to a new doctor, please put in a referral to a migraine/headache specialist at San Jose.

Thank you for your help,

Ivan

Dear Ivan,

I did send a referral to the neurology department and explained the history; they can always call me.

I am downsizing the general neurology part of my practice so it would be beneficial for Grace to find a neurologist closer to her home.

Let's be open to options.

I understand that it is frustrating to keep explaining her history, but sometimes new "eyes" are more helpful.

Sincerely,

Erika S. Weber MD.

"I assume Dr. Weber gave you the notes from my Stanford treatment?" The pulsing fluorescent lights in Kaiser San Jose's neurology department are doing nothing for my migraine.

Dr. Hassan stares through me blankly. "You were treated at Stanford, you say?" His white coat is firmly pressed and his thinning hair implies decades of experience, and possible impending retirement.

I nod.

Dr. Hassan squints back at the computer. "I don't see Stanford anywhere in your case history."

October 8th, 2020: Sixteen Needles

"Injections? Like, *head* injections?"

"Yes, in the head. Of course." Dr. Hassan is rustling through a stack of brochures in the metal cabinet next to his computer. "Usually, we try other things first, but right now you have migraine thirty out of thirty days. You only need migraine fifteen out of thirty days to qualify." He finds what he's looking for and passes me a brochure. "You can read more about the treatment here. Maybe send me a message and let me know what you want."

"So, you're saying these shots are the best recommendation you have?" Ivan looks skeptical.

"As I said, you can read more at home. But they're very safe. Very effective. I would give them to my wife."

I catch Ivan's eye and nod vigorously, or as vigorously as I can. At this point, I've had a migraine for eighty-four days. We've just been transferred back to Kaiser San Jose after spending two years at the elite Kaiser Redwood City and four months at the even more exclusive Stanford Medical Center. Our dream of finding a cure for my seizures might have faded with the summer, but we still hope a fresh neurologist will be able to tackle the migraine half of what's become a seizure-migraine disorder. My attempt at signaling that I *want* the injections must have failed because Ivan begins hedging.

"Yeah, I think we'll talk about it at home and get back to you. Thanks for the info and all, but head injections might be a tall order."

"I don't need to talk about it!" I interject. "I've been dying over here for over three months. I mean, it's not like I *want* shots in my head, but I'll take them."

The doctor hesitates, then follows my lead. "You are the patient. We will schedule it as follow-up since my assistant needs time to get the injections ready. We will see you in two, maybe three, days, then start treatment."

"Wonderful! I . . ."

"I do need to tell you these do not work the same on everybody. Some patients feel better immediately. Some it takes two, maybe three, rounds to see results. Some it does not work at all. But this is what we must try."

"*Rounds*?" Suddenly, the injections don't sound quite as appealing.

"Yes, rounds. We give injections every three months. If you do not see results after the third round, then we stop."

"Um . . . that seems like a lot." I can't imagine nine more months of a continuous migraine. "How often do they *not* work?"

'With a case as difficult as yours, I cannot say. Most patients do not have migraine thirty out of thirty days. But it's better to see the glass half full, yes?"

"Well . . . yes. Yes, I guess you're right." The doctor wouldn't know, but that's the secular version of what I've been writing about over the past three years. *And we know that God causes everything to work together for the good of those who love God and are called according to his purpose for them* (Rom. 8:28, NLT). When did I stop believing that? Was it after just an hour of sitting under fluorescent lights with a migraine? Or had I stopped believing it earlier?

Ivan must sense my distress. "Well, let's go ahead and schedule if Grace is sure she wants to go through with it. I'm off work since it's the summer, so we can come as soon as you're ready."

Head injections. The brochure describes the marvelous benefits (and "extremely uncommon" side effects), but fails to mention the number or exact location of the injections. I don't find its lack of specificity too concerning, however. This can't be worse than being hit by a car. "Injections" probably means two shots—at worst, no more than three.

But something seems wrong when the nurse calls me back to the exam room. "Don't you want your husband to come with you?" She looks concerned.

"You don't have to worry about me." I laugh. "I'm used to lots of needles."

"I think he should come with you." This is the first time a nurse has overridden a positive self-assessment. I gesture for Ivan to follow us. A little moral support might be nice, even if it seems like overkill for a couple of shots. Things only get stranger once I slide onto the exam table.

"Does ice sound good? Or numbing gel?"

"What?"

"We could also do both."

"I'm not sure I need . . .

"Trust me. You want at least one."

I will my drumming brain to cooperate, but it's moving on migraine speed as usual. All I know is I've never been offered painkiller for an injection. "It's just shots, right?"

"Why don't we go with the gel. We can always do ice later if you change your mind. Oh, and here's a hair tie. Do you mind pinning your hair up? Like, way up so doctor can see your neck." *Doctor can see your neck.* Something is absolutely wrong here.

Dr. Hassan shuffles in the room right after the nurse finishes rubbing the numbing gel across more of my forehead than I'd like. He dispenses with small talk and gestures to Ivan. "You want to hold her hand?" This unnerves me more than the gel. Neurologists are some of the least empathetic specialists I've experienced since my accident.

"Um . . . sure." Ivan is as surprised as I am. "Tell me where to go so I won't be in your way." The doctor indicates the left side of the table, then asks me to take off my glasses and lie down. I know better than to mention I can't feel Ivan holding my left hand.

And then the injections begin. *One. Two. Three. I made it!* Except the needle keeps going.

Four . . . Five . . . Six . . .

The doctor is asking Ivan and me all sorts of idiotic questions about Ivan's job, my accident, why we moved to San Jose. If it's supposed to be a distraction technique, it isn't working. I'm completely aware of the needle sliding in and out, sketching the migraine's perimeter on the left side of my face. Then Dr. Hassan switches to the right side where the migraine isn't. "Just in case," he explains. Finally, he asks me to sit up. Just as I'm about to stand, he clears his throat. "Can I see your neck?"

"But I don't have any pain in my neck."

"You see, the migraines, for some patients they come from the neck." I sigh and lower my head so he can reach the back of my neck, then I begin counting from where I left off.

Fourteen . . . Fifteen . . . Sixteen. Sixteen! So that's why nobody told me how many injections I would be getting. No one thinking rationally would agree to this. Well, maybe someone who'd had a migraine for eighty-seven days. I pray that the shots kick in immediately, and vow not to schedule the second round if they don't.

They don't. But Dr. Hassan convinces me to try the second round—and the third— before calling it a lost cause. Perhaps I agree because there aren't any other treatments. Perhaps it's because his honest, no-nonsense manner is different from my previous doctors', or because I'm personally biased. He taught at SUNY Syracuse before moving to California, and is familiar with Eastman.

My original round of injections took place in August 2019, followed by a second round in December, and a third in March 2020. The third round falls on my twenty-seventh birthday (which I do not tell the doctor), and we finally see results a couple of weeks later. Instead of lasting weeks at a time, the migraines only last two or three days. And they actually respond to pain medication. After two years of treatment, I still have more migraines than most people, but also enjoy several days each month free from pain.

Having a doctor to remind me that all things work together for good will stick with me longer than the shock of getting sixteen shots when I'd bargained for only two. God had helped me build my post-accident life on the truth that He can use the worst experiences for His glory, but I'd lost sight of that. I had lost sight of it to such an extent that a person who (to my knowledge) didn't even follow God thought I needed help seeing the bright side. We all go through seasons of loneliness and grief, maybe even hopelessness. I'd be lying if I said the past few months haven't been extremely dark for me. But my prayer is that we can each survive and thrive by believing these seasons don't last forever. God has an end point and a purpose for each one.

I love this encouragement from the Apostle Paul: "The temptations in your life are no different from what others experience. And God is faithful. He will not allow the temptation to be more than you can stand. When you are tempted, he will show you a way out so that you can endure" (1 Cor. 10:13, NLT).

121

February 28th, 2021: Home Sweet Home

"I guess this could work. It's a tight fit, but I'm over being picky." Ivan and I are considering Option #1, a two-bedroom condo in our favorite complex, five minutes away from Kaiser, my parents' condo, and Ivan's job. The downside is showering within eighteen inches of the washing machine. I'm also not completely sold on a two-bedroom. We've thrived in one-bedrooms so far. And didn't we agree to *economize* when we began condo hunting? Still, it might be nice if Ivan had room for a baby grand. We sleep on it and text our realtor to make an offer the next morning. The condo is already sold.

The next weekend we mean business. It's already the end of January and we've told my parents we'll be out of the spare room we're renting from them by March. Assuming it takes thirty days to close, this is our last opportunity to find that elusive dream condo. But our hyper-specific needs, such as close proximity to my parents and first floor or ADA friendly, yield only two options. Option #2 is a lemon, although we try convincing ourselves otherwise. The condo is located in the same favorite complex as Option #1, but no amount of downsizing can make 560 square feet livable for two cats and two adults. Especially since one adult does not work or even go outside very much. "Just wait," our realtor smiles. "I think you might like the other one." I desperately hope she isn't pulling a *worse* → *better* = *sales job*.

She isn't.

This morning we woke up in Option #3, a two-bedroom that meets every one of our "needle in a haystack" specifications. Not only that, but the owners had updated the kitchen and bathroom just prior to selling the unit. Example: Our bathroom has a trendy, fleur-de-lis tile floor instead of the aforementioned micro-shower scenario. And the best part is the location. Ever since we moved to San Jose, Mom and Ivan have been driving me to a walking trail near a historic hotel called Hayes Mansion. We weren't sure, but Mom thought there was either a condo complex or a traditional neighborhood behind the mansion. *Wouldn't it be nice for Ivan and Grace to live there?* she'd often wonder. Ivan and I never gave it more than half a thought. If there were neighborhoods back there, they were probably expensive. We were wrong. Our new complex has a gate leading straight to the park.

I feel blessed—almost guilty—as I write. God would have been gracious to meet even some of our needs, or at least our truncated timeline. The fact that He went above and beyond, especially during COVID when loss and disappointment were widespread, is difficult to comprehend. On a human level, we're grateful to my parents for hosting us after the lease for our apartment expired. We're also grateful to my sister and her husband for helping us move since I can't handle boxes or clean the house very well. We couldn't have made it through last weekend without the four of them.

Ivan's Thoughts

The condo seems like a miracle. Against all odds, Grace and I own our own home in the Silicon Valley, an area with one of the highest costs of living in the United States. We're also making it on a single income from my job as a music teacher at a private school. Human odds are meaningless against God's sovereignty. God allows what He chooses—both good and evil.

God is not the source of evil. But evil entered our world and corrupted human nature after Adam and Eve rebelled against God. As their descendants, we've also rejected God, the holy and perfect source of eternal life. We've embraced sin, death, and decay. How amazing is it that our almighty Creator loved us enough to pay for our rebellion Himself? Because His Son Jesus died for our sins and rose from the grave, we

can enjoy reconciliation with God, a renewed spiritual life, and an eternity in heaven if we accept Jesus as our Savior.

But if God really loves His children so much, why did He allow the accident to happen to Grace? Why did He take away her treasured violin? Why doesn't God heal her completely?

These questions plague the back of my mind. They are reasonable. They are natural responses to pain, loss, trauma. And they lead to darkness if I choose to dwell on them.

Instead, I dwell in the light of God's goodness and love. By God's grace, I believe that He is calling me and Grace to our final home in the new heavens, where we will dwell with Him for eternity in perfect peace and joy. All the pain and suffering we're experiencing in this world will become mere shadows that serve to offset the glorious bliss of being completely rescued from brokenness, sin, and death.

Everyone believes something about death. Even believing nothing happens after death is still believing something. Paul taught the Christians in Thessalonica:

"For since we believe that Jesus died and rose again, even so, through Jesus, God will bring with him those who have fallen asleep . . . Then we who are alive, who are left, will be caught up together with them in the clouds to meet the Lord in the air, and so we will always be with the Lord" (1 Thess. 4:14-17).

This is what Scripture teaches Christians about life after death. As we look honestly at our own hearts, we should ask ourselves why we believe what we believe.

Grace's accident continually reminds her and me that the God of the Bible is real, sovereign, and worthy of all worship and obedience. God's Word is an unshakable foundation that has sustained us through indescribable chaos. No matter what our earthly future holds, Grace and I are homeward bound.

May 30, 2021: The Healing Power of Music

My sister, Anna, is a gifted pianist. She won regional and state competitions from the time she was in elementary school, and even spent a couple of years in high school at the internationally renowned Colburn School of Music in Los Angeles, California.

I am not a gifted pianist. This is not for lack of opportunity or motivation: I attended all Anna's lessons when I was living at home, and even took a year of my own private lessons in high school. Conservatory-bound instrumentalists are expected to have a decent knowledge of piano upon arrival or endure however many semesters of classes it takes to pass the proficiency exam. I played well enough to pass the exam. And then I quit.

A month after buying our condo, Ivan announced that it was time to find a piano for the second bedroom. The problem was we had no money. We had dreamt of a top-of-the-line Steinway, but those cost more than some luxury cars. Always the practical one, Ivan suggested tabling the Steinway for our hypothetically more lucrative middle age. He just wanted something that *works*. We settled for a 1925 Wurlitzer upright grand—respectable, but nothing to write home about.

A few weeks after we had hauled the Wurlitzer home, I began wondering if I could relearn piano even though I had failed with violin. Piano and violin are distinct because pianists can see both hands, while violinists can't see either. I can somewhat control my left hand if I'm looking at it, so I began tinkering with our piano's yellowed keys a few minutes every day. At first, I could only play five notes in a row, one hand at a time. A month later, I was able to practice thirty minutes a day, and I learned the first page of a sonata—hands together.

It seems impossible that I'm making music after years of disappointed resignation. This may not be the instrument I'd begged God for, but it's better than no instrument at all. Far better. And my left hand is even coordinated enough to play intermediate pieces. My progress is so startling that I'm not sure my family believes me. Then there's the blog: Am I ready for a plethora of reactions after I announce this near-miraculous turn of events? So, I play quietly from 7:00-7:30 each night, listening as the notes spill into the dusk and mingle with the crickets' thrumming chorus. But Ivan knows something is missing.

I studied music *performance*.

With a bit of encouragement, I learn a Russian piece called "Humoresque" by Rodion Schedrin. Humoresques represent little jokes, perfect for an amateur debut. One May morning, Ivan drives me to my parents' condo and positions his iPad on a tower of books, six feet in front of Mom's hundred-year-old grand piano. I sit at the bench, inhale deeply, arrange my fingers over the keys. Ivan hits *Record* and nods. My fingers begin their syncopated dance and then I am flying, swept away by the golden spirit of melody that's haunted me for twenty-two years. The video isn't perfect since I'm still learning to control both hands simultaneously. I don't care. This is my message to everyone I love: I'm alive, and I'm blessed. God's kept His promise to bring my music back to life, just as I journaled three years ago. I can't imagine what the future holds.

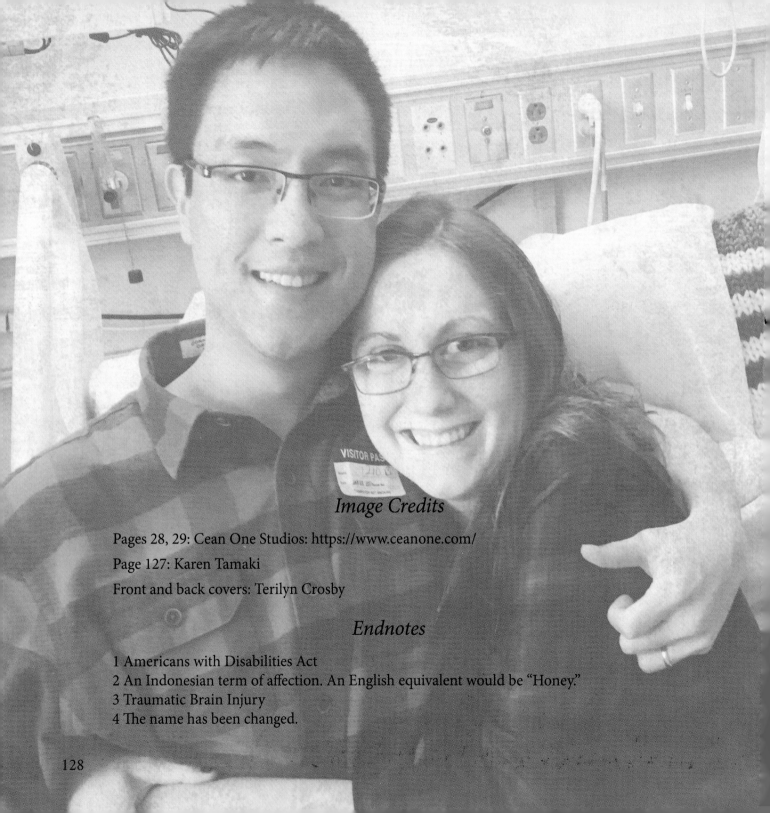

Image Credits

Pages 28, 29: Cean One Studios: https://www.ceanone.com/

Page 127: Karen Tamaki

Front and back covers: Terilyn Crosby

Endnotes

1 Americans with Disabilities Act
2 An Indonesian term of affection. An English equivalent would be "Honey."
3 Traumatic Brain Injury
4 The name has been changed.